GREECE

HISTORY AND TREASURES OF AN ANCIENT CIVILIZATION

WHITE STAR PUBLISHERS

CONTENTS

1
2
3
4
5

TEXTS
STEFANO MAGGI

EDITORIAL DIRECTOR
VALERIA MANFERTO DE FABIANIS

COLLABORATING EDITORS
LAURA ACCOMAZZO
GIORGIO FERRERO

GRAPHIC DESIGNER
PAOLA PIACCO

© 2007 White Star s.p.a.
Via Candido Sassone, 22/24
13100 Vercelli, Italia
www.whitestar.it

TRANSLATION: CATHERINE BOLTON

ISBN-10: 88-544-0202-8
ISBN-13: 978-88-544-0202-7

REPRINTS:
1 2 3 4 5 6   11 10 09 08 07

Color separation: Fotomec, Turin
Printed in China

1 - A HOPLITE IN BATTLE POSITION; 6TH CENTURY BC (STAATLICHE MUSEEN, BERLIN).

2-3 - THE ACROPOLIS AND THE PARTHENON, ATHENS.

4-5 - THE GOLD QUIVER FROM THE TOMB OF PHILIP II (ARCHAEOLOGICAL MUSEUM, SALONIKA).

6-7 - SCENE FROM THE TROJAN WAR ON A CUP BY THE BRYGOS PAINTER (THE LOUVRE, PARIS).

9 - THE NIKE OF SAMOTHRACE, ONE OF THE MASTERPIECES OF HELLENISTIC ART (THE LOUVRE, PARIS).

INTRODUCTION

Until only recently – and, for many, even now – Greek art and culture have been represented by and virtually circumscribed within the very narrow limits of an established and simple definition: classicism.

It is hard to determine exactly what "classical" means and the word is somewhat abused. "Classical" refers to everything that, ancient and modern, seems to please everyone. It is something that never ages, an ideal point of reference and source of inspiration, something with enduring attraction.

Greece, and chiefly Athens, was and is the epitome of "classicism" along with Rome, though earlier than Rome and to a greater extent. This is true despite the discovery of cultures far removed from the "classical" period in space and time, such as Knossos, Thera, Mycenae and Troy, Delphi, Olympia, Thermos, the island of Aegina, not to mention nearby Messenia, the enemy of Sparta, and Olynthus on the Chalcidian Peninsula. And then there are the very recent discoveries of the royal Macedonian tombs of Vergina! In essence, though the complexity of the "Greek phenomenon," its origins, historical development and the influence of other cultures (the Near East, Egypt and the Balkans) have clearly been demonstrated, the prevalent idea has been – and, for some, still is – that of an autonomous, absolute and crystalline creative movement: a sort of "Greek miracle" to which all of Western culture will be forever indebted. Yet the idea of the miracle has proven deceptive and dangerous.

For centuries it was thought that the common roots of the European world and its offshoots fully resided in Hellenism. The doges would proudly compare Venetian sea power to Sparta's leadership on land. During the French Revolution, the idea of

égalité was paralleled with the presumed equality typical of Spartan society (overlooking its harsh oligarchic nature and the exploited masses). The direct democracy of Athens, in which citizens voted by a show of hands, was long confounded with the modern representative democracies of the West, in which people vote by delegating power to representatives. In short, according to the great German philosopher Georg Wilhelm Friedrich Hegel, "The name of Greece strikes home to the hearts of men of education in Europe." Today, this no longer seems to be the case, because in a set of different societies that are increasingly characterized, influenced and transformed by the mingling of populations and culture, we no longer seek "common origins," the preeminence of a civilization or a "universal history." (Indeed, this "universe" cannot be Europe or the West!)

There is no doubt, however, that history as the arduous search (*historie*) for a problematic truth and as a methodical doubt – as opposed to the "certain" history written by the human hand through divine dictation and distinctive of the Eastern world – is a product of Greek thought. As a result, thanks to the thirst for knowledge of historians such as Herodotus, Thucydides and Polybius, the populations of Europe have shared the common fate of "entering history" at the point in which, around the Mediterranean, they encountered the Greek civilization and then the Roman one.

The figurative art of the Greeks long remained tied to the world of the gods, not unlike the millenary Oriental models. It was an art imbued with religious values. However, with respect to the models from which it could draw its inspiration, its great innovative merit – which is not always grasped by modern

10 - THIS GOLD ARTIFACT PORTRAYING HERACLES WITH THE LION'S SKIN IS FROM MOUND III AT KRALEVO, A THRACIAN NECROPOLIS DATING BACK TO THE 3RD CENTURY BC (HISTORY MUSEUM, TARGOVISHTE).

11 - THIS PORTRAIT OF THE GODDESS ATHENA WEARING A HELMET IS A COPY OF A STATUE BY THE SCULPTOR CEPHISODOTUS, THE FATHER OF PRAXITELES (THE LOUVRE, PARIS).

scholars, who instead focus on the perfection of techniques – was the move toward the human dimension and the humanization of figures. This was a process that, by bringing artwork closer to the human level, opened people's minds and educated them by imparting new sensitivity.

Because of everything we have said so far, the ancient Hellenes and their culture risk vanishing or being overshadowed, leaving behind a limited and conceptually superficial view of their importance. In short, their legacy is gradually being distorted or underestimated. The names of the plains of Marathon and the pass of Thermopylae, familiar to generations of students as the places symbolizing the *histoire bataille*; the sites of the stadium of Olympia and the sanctuary of Delphi evoking the inextricable link between religion and the competitive spirit of sportsmanship; and daily terms such as "political" (from *polis*, the city understood as the community of free men with the competition of ideals), "laconic" (from Laconia, the region of Sparta in which people were less loquacious than elsewhere) and "ostracism" (from *ostrakon*, the potsherd on which the citizens of Athens would write the name of a politician they wanted to expel) are becoming weak and stereotyped concepts that have little significance.

A question is repeated time and again. Is it still meaningful today to look toward the ancient Greeks in the hopes of gleaning some sort of lesson? Of course it is, but this must be done with renewed and critical attention, in order to grasp the essential meaning of the legacy they have given us "between East and West." This expression suggests that the Greeks have represented a spatial and temporal beachhead between the ancient civilizations of the Near East – Mesopotamia and Egypt – and those that would later develop in Europe. Thus, the Greeks must not necessarily be credited with a primacy, much less a miracle. We must merely acknowledge their unfailing desire and ability to experiment and open up new paths, impartially embracing the good things that other populations had to offer. The Greek alphabet, which could represent any expression of human thought using approximately 20 symbols, was borrowed from Phoenician writing, but the adaptation of this instrument – used for centuries for a Semitic language – to meet the needs of an Indo-European language such as Greek was ingenious.

Likewise, we can say that wisdom was not the prerogative of the Greeks (think of the Sapiential Books of the Bible), but philosophy (*philo sophia* means the love of wisdom or knowledge) as a science that studies nature, man and the relationship between the two – tense at times, fertile at others, and often mediated by reflections on the divine – is their creation. Can anyone remember the names of philosophers prior to Thales or Anaximander of Miletus?

Indeed, Miletus, the city in Hellenized Asia Minor, was a fundamental point of encounter, the crossroads for trade and cultural exchange between east and west.

Fundamentally, the Greek legacy contains many of the "things of man," ever poised between singular exemplariness and general historicity, between the awareness of one's own means or identity (with just a hint of a sense of superiority) and the generous cognizance that others also exist; a sense of otherness.

This book was written to generate an interest in the culture of ancient Greece, stimulate curiosity and kindle the desire to learn more, in order to grasp the historical experience of the Greeks in all its complexity, composed of extraordinary political, social, urbanistic and artistic insight but also of interdependence and borrowings from the cultural background of other populations. Its goal is to help bridge the gap between knowledge of the ancient ages and the use of antiquity. And to allow our culture to continue to view the Greeks as part of our past: in the words of the great anthropologist and historian Louis Gernet, *les Grecs sans miracle*.

THRACIA

PANAGYURISHTE ✦

BYZANTIUM ✦

PHRY

MACEDON

PELLA ✦

VERGINA ✦

OLYNTHUS ✦

TROY ✦

MYSIA

PERGAMUM ✦

LESBOS

LYDIA

EPIRUS

CORFU

THEBES ✦

EUBOEA

CHIOS

EPHESUS ✦

PRIENE ✦

CARIA

DELPHI ✦

CORINTH ✦

ATHENS ✦

DELOS

MILETUS ✦

MYCENAE ✦

EPIDAURUS ✦

SAMOS

OLYMPIA ✦

ARGOS ✦

HALICARNASSUS

MANTINEA ✦

TEGEA ✦
SPARTA ✦

ROME ✦

CUMA ✦

POSEIDONIA ✦

TARENTUM ✦

MAGNA
GRAECIA

SEGESTA ✦

SELINUS ✦

SICILY

AGRIGENTUM ✦

RHEGION ✦

SYRACUSE ✦

MILOS

AKROTIRI ✦

RHODES

MALLIA ✦

KNOSSOS ✦

CRETE

MEDITERRANEAN SEA

CYRENE ✦

16-17 - The Temple of Concord at
Agrigentum is one of the best-
preserved examples of Doric
architecture in Magna Graecia
(440 BC).

18-19 - This banquet scene was
painted on one of the panels that
covered the walls of the Tomb of
the Diver in Paestum, AD 480
(National Archaeological Museum,
Paestum).

BLACK SEA

BYTHINIA

PONTUS

CAPPADOCIA

LYCIA

CILICIA

ANTIOCH ◆

ISSUS ◆

◆ TRYSA

CYPRUS

SIDON ◆

TYRE ◆

ALEXANDRIA ◆

MEMPHIS ◆

EGYPT

THE ORIGINS
(3500-1000 BC)

The Neolithic culture of Sesklo and Dimini in Thessaly (4th-3rd millennium BC) and the Minoan civilization in Crete between 2500 and 1400 BC mark the history of the Greek peninsula before the arrival of the Indo-Europeans (the Achaeans) in about 1900 BC. They imposed a form of political superiority on the Pre-Greeks, which led to the rise of the Mycenaean civilization between 1600 and 1150 BC. The great movement of populations that involved the Mediterranean basin in about 1200 led to the arrival of the Dorians in the Greek peninsula (1100 BC).

THE ARCHAIC PERIOD
(1000-500 BC)

The end of the "dark centuries" (11th-10th centuries BC) ushered in the Archaic period. The 9th century marked a resurgence from the stagnant conditions that had affected the Greek continent. The *polis* became consolidated, the use of writing spread and the great colonization movement began (ca. 750 BC). Draco's Laws date from about 620 and Solon's timocratic reforms of 594 represented Athens' first steps toward democracy. The 6th century was one of tyrannies, including the Athenian tyranny of Peisistratus (564-527) and his sons (Hippias was expelled from the city in 510). Cleisthenes' democratic reforms (508) closed the Archaic period.

THE CLASSICAL PERIOD
(500-323 BC)

The Classical period opened with the Ionian Revolt (499-494) and the two Persian Wars (490 and 480). The victories at Plataea and Cape Mycale in 479 marked the Greeks' triumph over the Persians. The year 478 saw the establishment of the Delian-Attic League, a cornerstone for Athenian imperialism during the Age of Pericles (461-430). Work to construct the

Parthenon in Athens began in 448-447. The Peloponnesian War between Athens and Sparta devastated Greece from 431 to 404. This was also the period of the plague in Athens (430), the Peace of Callias (421), Athens' tragic expedition to Sicily (which ended in terrible defeat in 415-413), and the return of the oligarchy to Athens with the Council of 400 (411). In 404-403, following the rule of the Thirty Tyrants, Athens rebelled and democracy was restored. Spartan hegemony, in the wake of the tragic events that struck Athens at the end of the 5th century, was replaced by Theban domination (371-362): the Battle of Mantinea, which drew the war to a close, also marked the demise of the *polis* system. In 359 Philip II became the king of Macedon and in 338 he defeated the Greeks at the Battle of Chaeronea. The reign of Alexander the Great from 336 to 323 dramatically changed the historical, economic, social and cultural conditions of the Greek world.

HELLENISM
(323-31 BC)

Following the Diadochoi and Epigoni, Macedon's domination of Greece was transformed into full-fledged occupation in 262 with the Chremonidean War. The Peace of Naupactus (217) between Macedon and the Achaean League, on the one hand, and the Aetolic League and Sparta, on the other, ushered in a period of terrible crisis. In the meantime, Roman power was looming on the horizon. In 197 T. Quinctius Flamininus defeated the Macedonians at Cynoscephalae, and in 196 he proclaimed Greece's independence, turning it into a Roman protectorate. The Battle of Pydna put an end to Macedonian domination (168). With the capture of Corinth in 146 by Lucius Mummius, Greece became a Roman province. Athens was drawn into the power struggles among Roman generals of the Late Republic and was sacked by Sulla in 86. Following the Battle of Philippi (42), Augustus placed the mark of imperial power on the Acropolis in Athens by building a temple dedicated to the cult of Rome and Augustus (19 BC).

HISTORY AND TREASURES OF AN ANCIENT CIVILIZATION

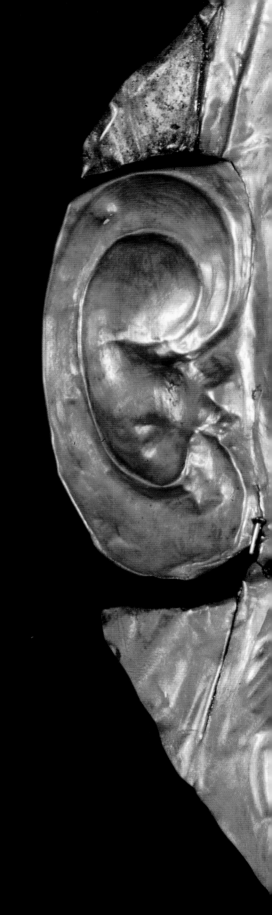

THE ORIGINS

20-21 - Heinrich Schliemann found the Mask of Agamemnon, made of gold foil, in Tomb V of Grave Circle A at Mycenae; ca. 1580-1550 BC (National Archaeological Museum, Athens).

22 - Abstractness is the distinctive feature of the Cycladic marble figurines from the Neolithic period; 2800-2200 BC (The Louvre, Paris).

23 top - The figurine of the harp player from Keros is one of the most famous works of Cycladic art; ca. 2200-2000 BC (National Archaeological Museum, Athens).

23 bottom - The schematic image of this female idol from Chalandriani, Syros, is virtually cut into the marble: only the breasts are modeled, whereas the arms and genitals are simply incised; 2000-1900 BC (National Archaeological Museum, Athens).

Greece's earliest historical events can be dated based on the relationships of the inhabitants of Hellas with the outside world: the Orient in general, but particularly Crete, Asia Minor and Egypt. True chronological tradition commences with the 8th century BC (by convention, the date of first Olympiad has been established as 776 BC), whereas only rough datings are possible for earlier periods. Even today, the terms of the periodization of the Early, Middle and Late Helladic vary enormously: Early Helladic (EH) 2600/2400 to 2000/1900 BC; Middle Helladic (MH) 2000/1900 to 1700/1550 BC; Late Helladic (LH) 1700/1550 to 1150/1100 BC.

No scholar has shed more light on the problem of the start of the Greek civilization than the Athenian historian Thucydides. In the 5th century BC, he wrote:

[I]t is evident that the country now called Hellas had in ancient times no settled population; on the contrary, migrations were of frequent occurrence, the several tribes readily abandoning their homes under the pressure of superior number. Without commerce, without freedom of communication either by land or sea, cultivating no more of their territory than the exigencies of life required....

At the beginning of the Middle Helladic, the Indo-Europeans reached the easternmost of the three large Mediterranean peninsulas. They did not arrive in a single migratory wave, but through the slow and intermittent influx of tribes and groups. According to tradition, the two oldest groups were the Achaeans and the Ionians, whereas the Aeolians and the Dorians represented the other two tribes.

The Indo-European element introduced forms of political supremacy to the area's Mediterranean populations – the Pre-Greeks – and in the Late Helladic this led to the rise of the Mycenaean civilization. Following a long period of prosperity, the decline of the Mycenaeans was accelerated by the migration of the Dorians, who descended into the Peloponnesus as part of a large movement of populations that involved the entire Mediterranean basin, starting in about 1200 BC. The arrival of the Achaeans in approximately 1900 and of the Dorians toward 1100 led to periods of cultural stagnation. Nevertheless, both groups – centuries apart – assimilated the heritage of the cultures they encountered (Pre-Greek, Minoan, Phoenician and Near Eastern) and adapted them to create a new and original one.

Most scholars have focused on the historic age – to the detriment of studies on Greek prehistory – and methodical research into the earlier phases has been conducted only recently. The points of reference for the Greek Neolithic are Sesklo (4th millennium) and Dimini (3rd millennium), in Thessaly. At these sites, archeologists have discovered early villages surrounded by defensive walls. These villages were characterized initially by huts and subsequently by houses with several rooms and a courtyard, culminating with the advent of the rectangular megaron, with a tripartite layout, a columned porch, a chamber with a hearth and a back area. This culture was distinguished by a rich array of incised or painted ceramics with red or brown decorations, and terracotta figurines (inspired by the widespread mother-goddess motif), revealing close relations with the Balkan and Anatolian areas. Specifically, contacts with Anatolia, through the islands and the Balkans, paved the way for the transition to the Metal Age in Greece, in an environmental setting that continued to be profoundly rural.

Instead, toward 2500 BC Crete evolved notably on a cultural level, taking part in the kind of development observed in Egypt and the great cities of Mesopotamia, and attaining a pre-urban organization.

THE MINOAN CIVILIZATION

The Minoan civilization (named for Minos, the legendary king of Crete) spanned the period from the middle of the 3rd millennium to about 1400 BC, or the entire Bronze Age. Its history has been reconstructed almost exclusively through archaeological documentation, because the texts written in the script known as "Linear A" have yet to be deciphered, due also to the fact that they pertain to a non-Greek language. Moreover, the sources written by coeval cultures provide little information about Crete. The history of the island has been influenced by its rapport with the sea. Its geographical location gave it control over sea routes and trade, permitting the exchange of goods and cultural experiences. This laid the groundwork for forms of hegemony that ancient historians referred to as thalassocracy (rule of the sea) when writing about Minos. An initial period of splendor toward the end of the 3rd millennium was characterized by the development of urban settlements in fertile areas and near the sea (Phaistos, Zakro, Mallia). These settlements were composed of large houses with several rooms, and interconnected common areas (Pre-palatial period). After an abrupt halt in growth toward 1700 BC, possibly due to natural disasters or — less likely — to internal conflicts or the impact of migrations from the East (the Hyksos invasion of Egypt), these settlements were rapidly rebuilt in more complex and monumental forms with a clearly palatial appearance in Phaistos, Mallia, Gournia, Hagia Triada and, above all, Knossos. The Palatial period, which lasted until the middle of the 2nd millennium, is famous for these building complexes, which were arranged around a vast courtyard. They had a series of rooms used for ceremonial and religious purposes, as service areas, and as storage for provisions and equipment. They were laid out on several levels without applying any axial or symmetrical criteria, creating a fluid and dramatic rapport with the rugged terrain. The most distinctive aspect of these structures was the effect of light and shadow created through the sequences and connections of open and enclosed spaces, and the series of porticos, doors and windows. This type of "anarchic" layout of the palaces is also suggested by the celebrated myth of the labyrinth at Knossos, from which the Athenian Theseus managed to escape only by following Ariadne's thread.

Art — painting in particular — rose to extraordinary heights. The walls of the palaces were richly decorated with frescoes

24 LEFT - AT KNOSSOS, THE PALATIAL SECTOR NEAR THE SOUTH PROPYLAEUM IS DECORATED WITH LARGE STYLIZED STONE HORNS THAT ARE BOTH ORNAMENTAL AND APOTROPAIC; 1650-1400 BC.

24 BOTTOM - THE NORTH ENTRANCE OF THE PALACE OF KNOSSOS IS MARKED BY A MASSIVE PORCH SUSTAINED BY COLUMNS THAT TAPER TOWARDS THE BOTTOM AND ARE PAINTED RED.

24-25 - THE SOUTH PROPYLAEUM OF THE PALACE OF KNOSSOS CONVEYS SUBTLE MONUMENTALITY THAT BLENDS WITH THE NATURAL SURROUNDINGS, UNDERSCORED BY THE FRESCO PORTRAYING OFFERING BEARERS.

26-27 - The crushed relief of a bull, sculpted in colored plaster, is the focal point of the north entrance of the Palace of Knossos.

28-29 - The overall view of the Palace of Knossos demonstrates the arrangement of blocks of rooms without any order or criteria of symmetry, one of the distinctive features of Crete's palatial architecture.

28 bottom left - The throne room has an alabaster throne, and the walls are elegantly frescoed with griffins.

whose quality is comparable to those of the Italian Renaissance. Most of these works turned to nature as a subject, but the artists were also highly imaginative. Landscapes populated with magnificent animals or youthful human figures, often painted in surreal colors, alternated with "historical" scenes of ships setting sail from bustling harbors or tableaux of religious ceremonies, acrobatic games and processions. A polychrome palette and accurate references to nature – particularly marine life – can also be found in pottery decorations, terracotta figurines, and relief work in stone and metal. This art also influenced the Aegean islands. The Cyclades and particularly Thera (modern-day Santorini) have also yielded extraordinary examples of large mural paintings.

28 BOTTOM RIGHT - NATURALISM AND BRILLIANT COLORS ARE THE HALLMARKS OF MINOAN FRESCOES.

29 TOP - A MAGNIFICENT FRESCO WITH BLUE DOLPHINS DECORATES THE MAIN ROOM OF THE QUEEN'S APARTMENT.

29 CENTER - ONE OF THE CONSTANT ELEMENTS OF MINOAN ARCHITECTURE WAS THE CAREFULLY PLANNED ARRANGEMENT OF SOURCES OF LIGHT, COURTYARDS AND – AS SHOWN HERE – LARGE PORCHES.

29 BOTTOM - COURTYARDS AND MONUMENTAL STAIRCASES CONNECTED AND ILLUMINATED THE CENTRAL AREAS OF THE PALACES, WHICH WERE SET ON DIFFERENT LEVELS.

The Minoan experience – with contributions from Egypt, Phoenicia, Anatolia and Syria – was assimilated by the Mycenaeans and influenced Greek art. One of the most important aspects of the cultural fusion following the Mycenaean colonization of Crete (approximately 1450) was the adoption of Minoan syllabic writing (Linear A) and the creation of Linear B (suitable for writing a Greek language). Michael Ventris and John Chadwick deciphered Linear B in the 1950s, making it possible to read thousands of tablets discovered at Knossos, and expanding our knowledge of the Mycenaean political, economic and social system.

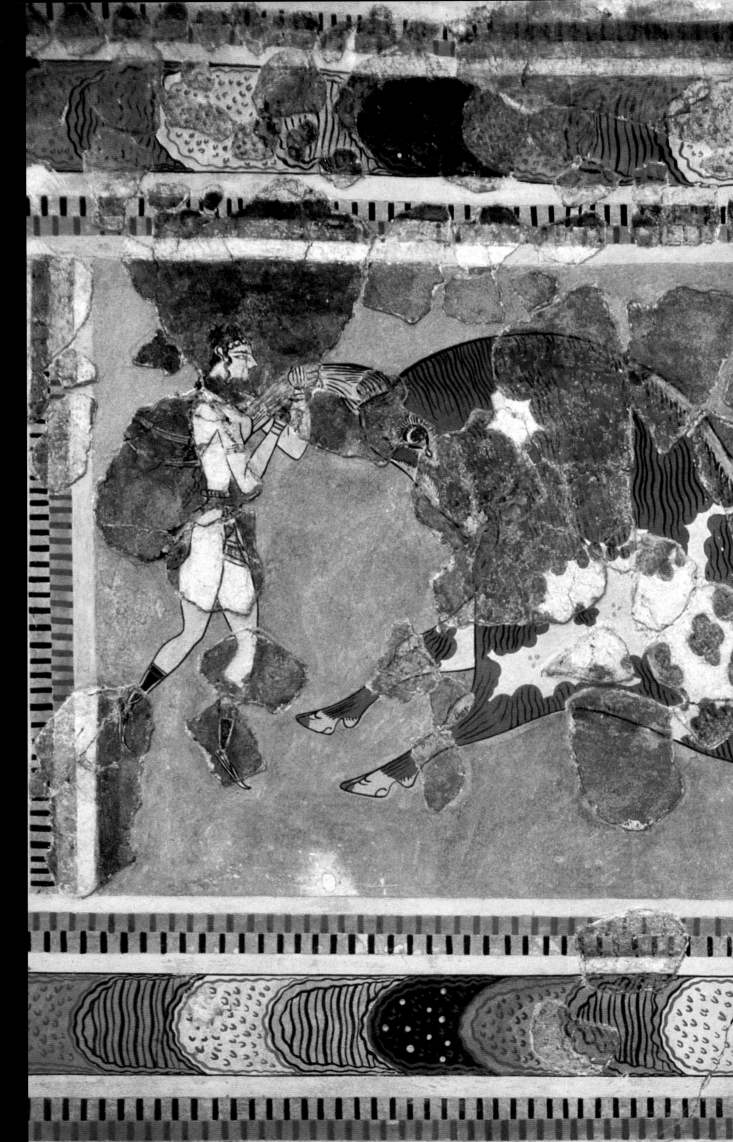

30-31 - This extraordinary fresco depicting the acrobatics of a young man on the back of a bull (taurokathapsia) is from the east sector of the Palace of Knossos (Archaeological Museum, Heraklion).

32 LEFT – THE PAINTED BAS-RELIEF STUCCO FIGURE KNOWN AS "THE PRINCE OF THE LILIES", EXPRESS AN EXQUISITE NATURALISTIC STYLE, WAS DISCOVERED AT THE PALACE OF KNOSSOS; CA. 1500 BC (ARCHAEOLOGICAL MUSEUM, HERAKLION).

32 RIGHT – THE FRESCO OF "THE BOXING CHILDREN" IS FROM THERA; CA. 1500 BC (NATIONAL ARCHAEOLOGICAL MUSEUM, ATHENS).

33 – THE KNOSSOS "WATER BEARER" IS

WITHOUT ILLUSIONISTIC RELIEF.

34-35 – THE FRESCO OF THE "BLUE LADIES" IS FROM THE THRONE ROOM AT KNOSSOS; CA. 1600 BC (ARCHAEOLOGICAL MUSEUM, HERAKLION).

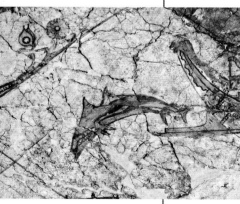

36 LEFT - THIS DOLPHIN IN
FRONT OF THE PROW OF A
WARSHIP IS FROM A FRESCO
AT THE WESTERN HOUSE
IN AKROTIRI, AND IT CONVEYS
THE NATURALISTIC CHARM OF
CYCLADIC ART; 16TH CENTURY
BC (NATIONAL ARCHAEOLOGICAL
MUSEUM, ATHENS).

36 RIGHT - THE FRESCO
OF THE YOUNG FISHERMAN
IS FROM THE WESTERN
HOUSE AT AKROTIRI,
WHICH MAY HAVE BEEN THE
RESIDENCE OF A NAVAL
COMMANDER (NATIONAL
ARCHAEOLOGICAL MUSEUM,
ATHENS).

38 top - The high quality of Minoan jewelry is beautifully illustrated by the gold pendant with bees bearing a honeycomb; from Mallia, ca. 16th century BC (Archaeological Museum, Heraklion).

38 bottom - The steatite rhyton from Knossos, a vase carved in the shape a bull's head, conveys an extraordinary natural quality; ca. 1500 BC (Archaeological Museum, Heraklion).

39 - The famous faïence figurine in lively colors represents the Snake Goddess and is from a cult room at the Palace of Knossos; 1600-1580 BC (Archaeological Museum, Heraklion).

Shortly after the middle of the 2nd millennium – once again, after several catastrophes (including the eruption of a volcano on the island of Thera – Cretan power was weakened and the island was invaded by Achaean groups from the Greek mainland: the Mycenaeans.

Between 1400 and 1200 BC, the golden age of the Mycenaean civilization, political power was not centralized, but was shared by several autonomous cities: Mycenae and Tiryns in Argolis, Pylos in Messenia, Thebes and Orchomenus in Boeotia, Athens in Attica, and Iolcus in Thessaly. These areas did not have extensive territorial holdings and were linked by a common culture. Life revolved around the palace, which reflected a different architectural conception with respect to the Minoan one, as it was more compact and centered on the *megaron*, or the royal audience room with a hearth in the middle. The king (*wanax*), who headed the ruling class of warriors

and noble landowners (*lawoi*), held civil and religious powers, whereas the "leader of the *lawoi*" (*lawagetas*) served as the military commander. The rural districts (*damoi*) were governed by the palace, which – together with the dignitaries' residences – was surrounded by sturdy walls. The limited space in the citadel thus required a compact and organic layout for the palace, the focal point of which was a courtyard with a monumental entrance or *propylaeum*, and a *megaron*. There was a porch in front of the *megaron*, which in turn was characterized by a central round hearth surrounded by four columns, and a throne on the right side. The architectural model of the *megaron* and its simple compositional language originated from the mainland rather than Aegean layouts. This basic plan incorporated Minoan elements, such as porches and *propylaea*, as well as decorative elements, chiefly paintings portraying processions and heraldic animal motifs (lions and griffins).

41 - THE GOLD RHYTON IN THE SHAPE OF A LION'S HEAD WAS PART OF THE RICH FURNISHINGS FROM THE ROYAL TOMBS OF GRAVE CIRCLE A; 16TH CENTURY BC (NATIONAL ARCHAEOLOGICAL MUSEUM, ATHENS).

40 LEFT - THE LONG *DROMOS*, PARTIALLY EXCAVATED IN ROCK, SERVED AS THE CORRIDOR LEADING TO THE *THOLOS* OF AEGISTUS AT MYCENAE; 1500-1460 BC.

40 RIGHT - THE CUP OF NESTOR, DECORATED WITH TWO DOVES ON THE HANDLES, IS ONE OF THE PRICELESS OBJECTS THAT HEINRICH SCHLIEMANN UNEARTHED IN GRAVE CIRCLE A AT MYCENAE; 16TH CENTURY BC (NATIONAL ARCHAEOLOGICAL MUSEUM, ATHENS).

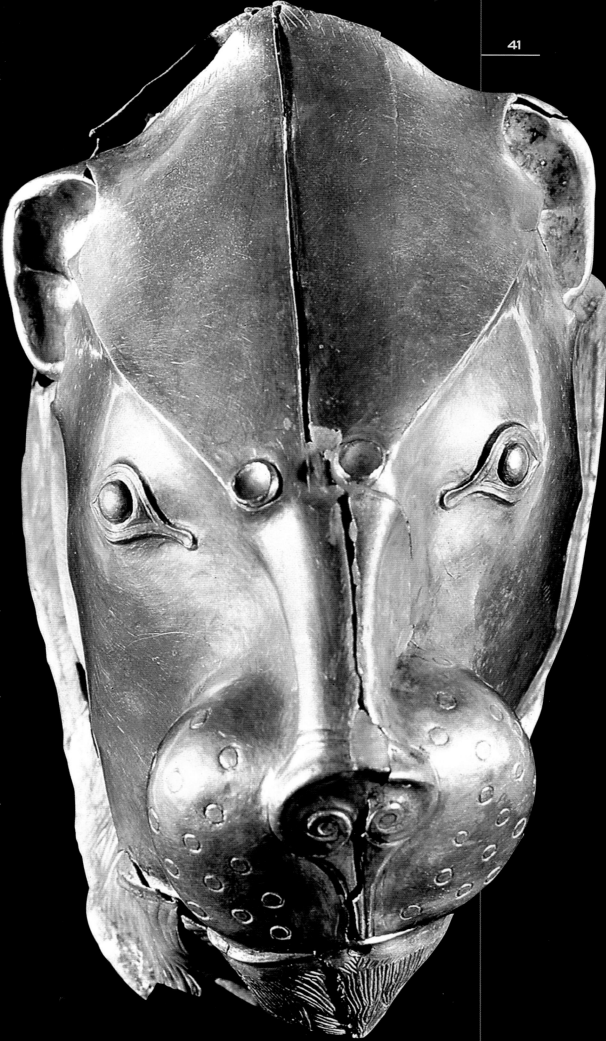

The necropolises of these well-organized centers attest to substantial wealth and artistry, particularly in comparison with the unexceptional level of the Helladic culture. The burial sites discovered at Mycenae, known as Grave Circles A and B, are excellent examples of this cultural level. The burials have yielded well-known gold burial masks, as well as swords with blades decorated with narrative scenes in damascened work and niello, vases shaped like animal heads, and rings made of precious metals. However, it is difficult to distinguish imported pieces from locally produced objects. The oldest burials of Grave Circle A (late 17th – early 16th century), which were shaft graves, held the remains of members of the royal family. In the 14th century, the burial grounds were enclosed within the defensive walls of the citadel, probably because the deceased had become the object of a particular cult. Grave Circle B, which dates back to the 17th century, was outside the citadel. It was probably created for a cadet branch of the royal family and was distinguished by simple burials in bare earth, with stelae as markers. It was subsequently reused during the first half of the 16th century, and these burials were accompanied by extremely rich accoutrements. Following the introduction (16th century) of chamber tombs, excavated in rock and used for families (possibly reflecting Egyptian influence), one of the most significant forms of Mycenaean architecture appeared: the *tholos* or beehive tomb. This type of mortuary structure consisted of a circular chamber, cut into the hillside, with a false dome roof covered by a tumulus and approached via a long entrance corridor (*dromos*). It was still in use during the 15th century, and the Treasury of Atreus and the Tomb of Clytemnestra, built in the 14th century, represent the acme of this type of burial.

In general, Mycenaean art was profoundly influenced by Minoan art, as can clearly be seen in pottery, whose decorative patterns initially drew heavily on the organic motifs of Crete (plants, flowers and marine life). The progressive simplification and schematization of subjects went hand in hand with the development of hunting and war scenes. A trend toward abstraction emerged during the final phase of production, and in Mycenae (13th century), this culminated with what is referred to as the "Granary style," distinguished by simple wavelike lines. There are very few small sculptures, with the exception of a few exquisite ivory figurines. Ivory, which was imported from Syria, was also carved to make pommels for swords, mirror handles and small jewelry boxes.

42-43 - In 1876 Heinrich Schliemann excavated the tombs of Grave Circle A, which contained priceless furnishings that are now displayed at the National Archaeological Museum in Athens.

42 top - The false dome roof of the *Tholos* of Atreus is a masterpiece of Mycenaean architecture; 13 century BC.

42 bottom - The techniques of damascening using gold and silver and of niello work are evident in these daggers depicting racing felines and a lion hunt, from Tomb VI of Grave Circle A at Mycenae; 16th century BC (National Archaeological Museum, Athens).

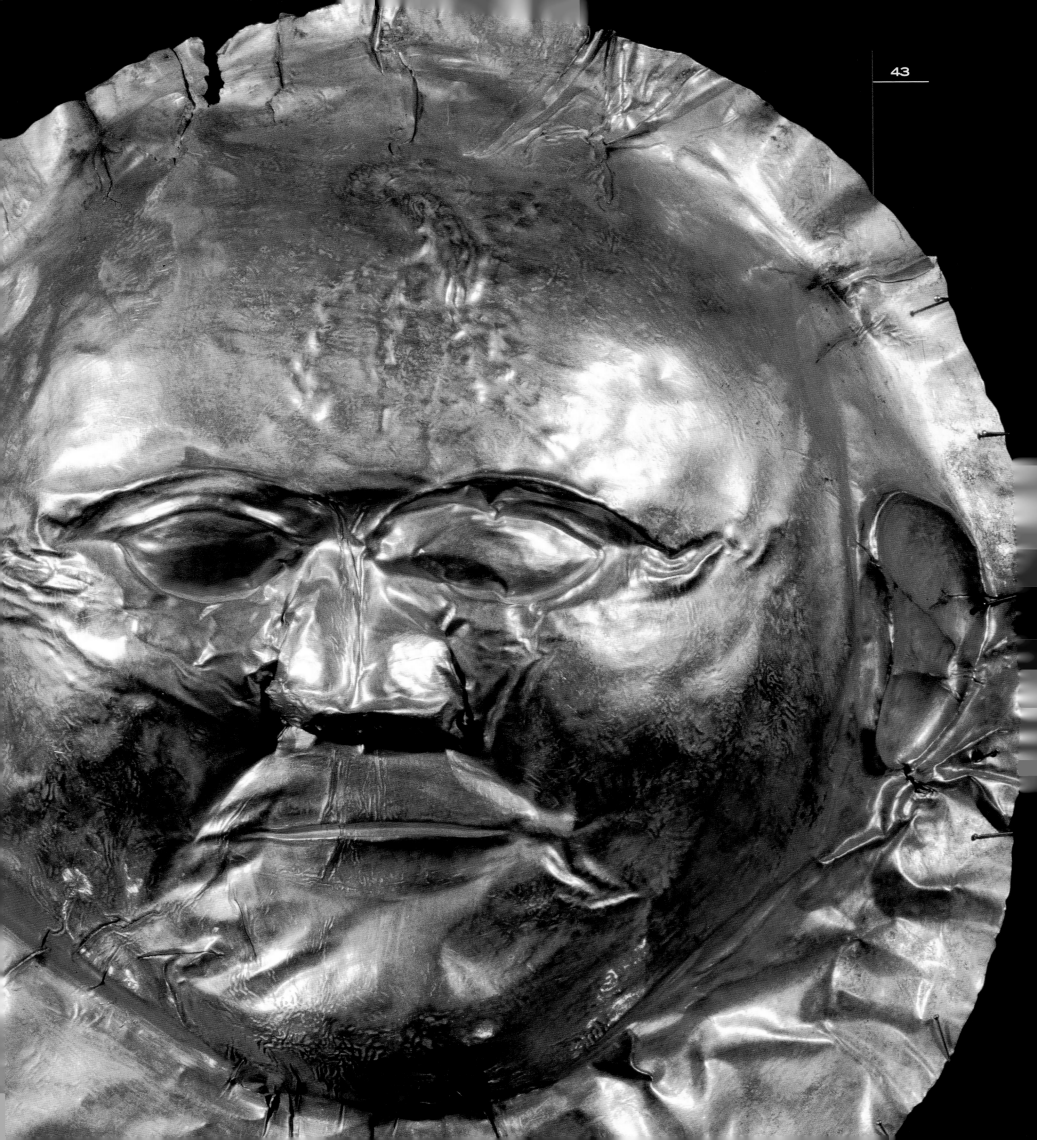

44 CENTER - THE FAMOUS GOLD CUPS FROM THE *THOLOS* AT VAPHIO, NEAR SPARTA, ARE DECORATED WITH *REPOUSSÉ* WORK DEPICTING THE CAPTURE AND TAMING OF BULLS; 15TH CENTURY BC (NATIONAL ARCHAEOLOGICAL MUSEUM, ATHENS).

44 BOTTOM - THE HEXAGONAL GOLD-PLATED BOX DECORATED WITH FLORA AND FAUNA IS ALSO FROM GRAVE CIRCLE A AT MYCENAE; 16TH CENTURY BC (NATIONAL ARCHAEOLOGICAL MUSEUM, ATHENS).

45 - THIS CLOSE-UP OF THE *REPOUSSÉ* WORK ON ONE OF THE VAPHIO CUPS CONVEYS THE EXCELLENT SENSE OF COMPOSITION AND DYNAMISM DISTINCTIVE OF MYCENAEAN CRAFTSMANSHIP (NATIONAL ARCHAEOLOGICAL MUSEUM, ATHENS).

44 TOP - THIS GOLD SIGNET RING FROM TIRYNS REPRESENTS A SCENE IN WHICH MONSTROUS CREATURES PAY HOMAGE TO AN ENTHRONED DEITY; 15TH CENTURY BC (NATIONAL ARCHAEOLOGICAL MUSEUM, ATHENS).

EXPANSION AND THE TROJAN WAR

Mycenaean expansion was concentrated in the eastern Mediterranean area and on the Anatolian coasts. There are also numerous traces of trade settlements, ports of call and emporia in Cyprus and on the Syrian coasts. However, the Mycenaeans also ventured westward in search of natural resources, reaching Sicily and southern Italy, Sardinia, the Iberian peninsula and North Africa. The events that altered the political geography of the eastern Mediterranean in the late 13th and early 12th centuries, triggered by raids by the "Sea People," had a profound effect on the Mycenaean world. The new international scenario gave the Mycenaeans the opportunity to expand toward the Black Sea, which provided them easy access to the metal-rich regions of the Caucasus regions. The story of the Trojan War mentioned a great expedition to conquer the strategic waters of the Hellespont, organized by the Mycenaean princes of the peninsula and the Greek islands. The Trojan War traditionally represents the chronological and conceptual point of reference for Greek history. Ancient historiographers cited it as a watershed, and in Book I of his *History of the Peloponnesian Wars* Thucydides gave a concise and cogent account of the earliest events of his homeland, from the great crisis of the Mycenaean kingdoms to the foundation of the *polis* system. In addition to the Trojan War, he considered the "return of the Heraclids" — meaning the invasion of the Dorians — another cardinal event.

The late return of the Hellenes from Ilium [Troy] caused many revolutions, and factions ensued almost everywhere; and it was the citizens thus driven into exile who founded the cities…. [Eighty years after the fall of Troy] the Dorians and the Heraclids became masters of Peloponnese; so that much had to be done and many years had to elapse before Hellas could attain to a durable tranquility undisturbed by removals, and could begin to send out colonies, as Athens did to Ionia and most of the islands, and the Peloponnesians to most of Italy and Sicily and some places in the rest of Hellas. All these places were founded subsequently to the war with Troy. But as the power of Hellas grew, and the acquisition of wealth became more an object, the revenues of the states increasing, tyrannies were by their means established almost everywhere — the old form of government being hereditary monarchy with definite prerogatives — and Hellas began to fit out fleets and apply herself more closely to the sea.

46 - THE CLOSE-UP OF THE MYKONOS PITHOS, DECORATED WITH RELIEF WORK, SHOWS A FAREWELL SCENE, PROBABLY BETWEEN HECTOR AND ANDROMACHE, WITH YOUNG ASTYANAX, BENEATH THE WALLS OF TROY; CA. 650 BC (ARCHAEOLOGICAL MUSEUM, MYKONOS).

47 - THE SCENE ON THE NECK OF THE CYCLADIC PITHOS USES CONCISE AND IMMEDIATE LANGUAGE TO RECOUNT THE CAPTURE OF TROY THROUGH THE RUSE OF THE TROJAN HORSE; CA. 650 BC (ARCHAEOLOGICAL MUSEUM, MYKONOS).

48-49 AND 49 TOP - TRYSA, IN LYCIA, WAS THE SITE OF THE TOMB OF A LOCAL DYNASTY. DECORATED WITH STONE RELIEF WORK, IT DEPICTS MYTHOLOGICAL AND HISTORICAL SCENES; CA. 375 BC. THE SCENES OF THE BATTLE BETWEEN THE GREEKS AND THE TROJANS WERE INSPIRED BY THE MODELS OF GREAT GREEK ART FROM THE EARLY 4TH CENTURY BC (KUNSTHISTORISCHES MUSEUM, VIENNA).

49 BOTTOM - THE SCENE OF THE SIEGE OF TROY (ON THE WEST SIDE OF THE MONUMENT AT TRYSA) IS ARRANGED IN TWO REGISTERS TO SHOW THE EVENTS UNFOLDING INSIDE AND OUTSIDE THE CITY. THE STUDY OF SPACE IN THE GROUPS OF SOLDIERS SET ON SEVERAL LEVELS IS EXTRAORDINARY AND IS PROBABLY BASED ON HISTORICAL MODELS (KUNSTHISTORISCHES MUSEUM, VIENNA).

Following the initial signs of danger in the first half of the 13th century (Mycenae erected the massive fortifications of the Lion Gate), the close of the century brought catastrophe. All the most important Mycenaean centers – from Mycenae itself to Tiryns, Pylos and Iolcus – were destroyed and none of the palaces were rebuilt. Disaster not only struck the buildings themselves, but the entire economic and social system. The towns next to the few palaces that survived shrank dramatically. Athens was the only city that was unaffected by these events. As the palaces disappeared, so did writing, as it had been used for palace administration.

The drop in population ushered in a period of serious decline. Once again, it has been up to archaeology to document this scenario. Collective monumental tombs were replaced by individual tombs, simple trenches or more complex cist tombs (trenches lined and covered with uneven slabs of stone). However, pottery did not change. Moreover, objects demonstrating close contact with the Balkans and central Europe began to appear, chiefly lighter and more manageable swords ands shields, and leather armor that, in rare cases, was decorated with bronze or boar teeth. In the 12th century, the use of iron to forge utensils and weapons became increasingly common. The ritual of cremation also appeared.

All this has been interpreted as the product of a wave of invasions attributed to the Dorians. Nevertheless, the Dorian penetration is no longer considered the sole cause of the collapse of the Mycenaean civilization but a contributing factor that merely compounded a deep-seated internal crisis. As a result, the invasion was probably a result of the power vacuum left by the collapse of the palatial system. In effect, innovations such as the cist tomb and the use of iron have been reassessed by

historians, who have observed that this type of burial was not new by any means, and that the use of iron was actually influenced by technical contributions from Cyprus.

Pottery is the "index fossil" for reconstructing the general events of the Sub-Mycenaean period. The overall scenario was quite poor in terms of craft techniques. In Attica, however, several innovations such as the fast wheel, the brush and the compass, as well as better preparation of the clay and firing at higher temperatures, gave these objects a distinctive appearance. Vessel shapes, fewer in number but expertly crafted, were characterized by shiny glazes and simple decorations, with a tendency to simplify naturalistic motifs into geometric patterns and forms. Consequently, this type of pattern – and the entire historical period – is referred to as Protogeometric. Athens, which had not been drawn into the great upheavals of the era, became the driving force of this trend. The style probably spread from Attica across Greece and the islands, along with another important change in mortuary rituals: the transition from interment to cremation.

New vase shapes appeared, such as the *hydria,* the *oinochoe,* and the *kantharos.* The amphora was also extremely popular, as it could be used to hold the cremated remains of the dead.

By the 10th century, the stagnant conditions of the Greek mainland tapered off and trade was gradually revived, bringing with it contacts with the eastern Mediterranean. Tomb furnishings from this period also testify to growing wealth. It is important to note that during the dark centuries, fundamental cultural elements such as alphabetic writing, which differed from Mycenaean syllabic script, began to develop. Above all, on a political and social level, the city came to replace the palace.

50 - GRAVE CIRCLE A IS SITUATED TO THE RIGHT OF THE ENTRANCE TO THE CITADEL OF MYCENAE, AND BUILDING N IS ON THE LEFT. THE BUILDING PROBABLY HOUSED BARRACKS FOR THE GARRISON OF THE STRONGHOLD, PROTECTED BY FORTIFIED RAMPARTS.

51 - ON THE LION GATE AT MYCENAE, AN ENORMOUS SCULPTED SLAB ENCLOSES THE DISCHARGING TRIANGLE OVER THE LINTEL: THE LION MOTIF CLEARLY HAS A PROTECTIVE PURPOSE; 13TH CENTURY BC.

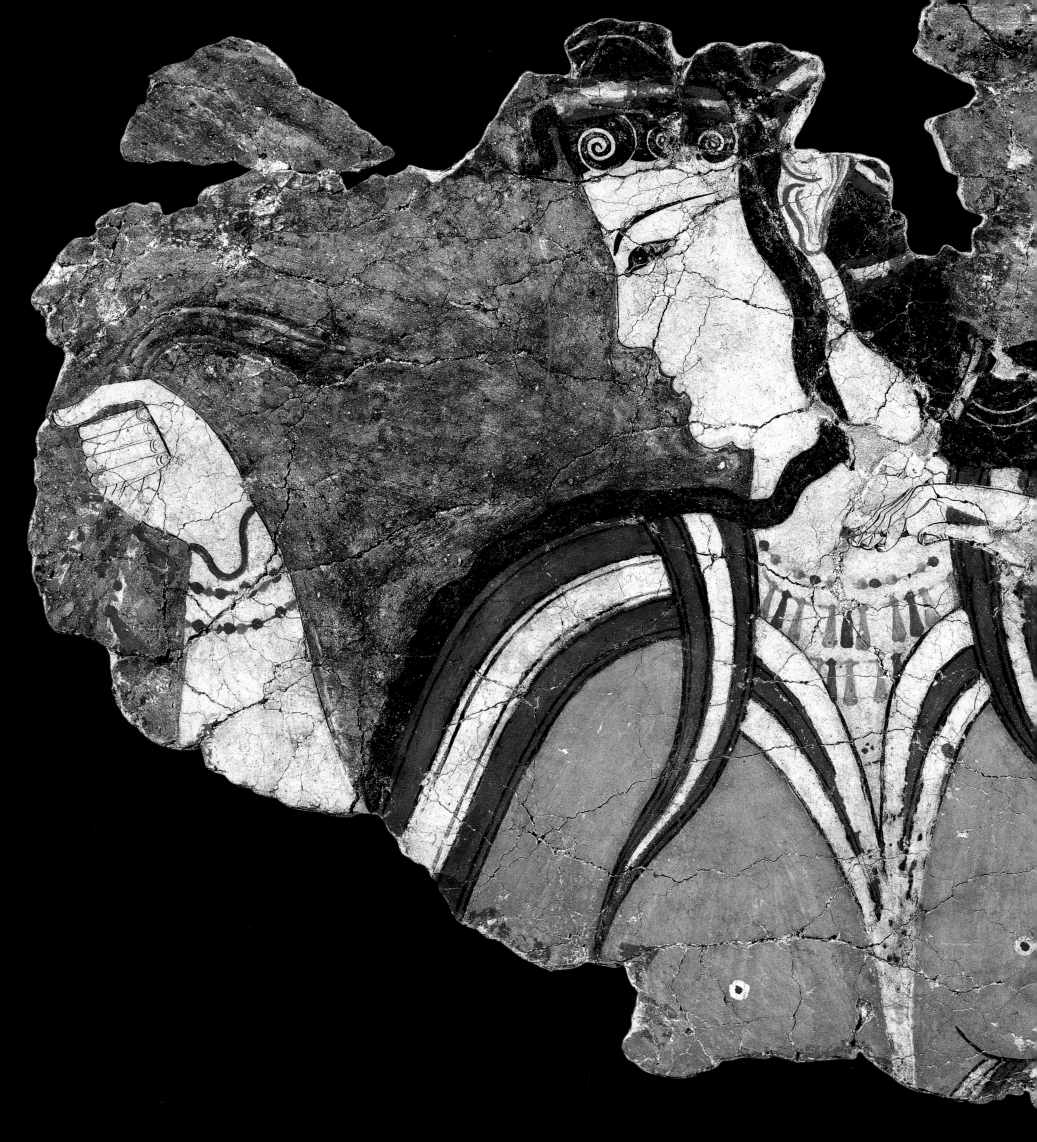

52-53 - THE "MYCENAEAN LADY" REPRESENTS ONE OF THE MOST EXQUISITE WORKS OF LATE MYCENAEAN PAINTING, DUE TO THE QUALITY OF ITS DESIGN AND ITS COLORS; 13TH CENTURY BC (NATIONAL ARCHAEOLOGICAL MUSEUM, ATHENS).

53 - THIS FRESCO FRAGMENT FROM KNOSSOS, REFERRED TO AS THE "PARISIAN LADY", DEPICTS A YOUNG CRETAN WOMAN WHO WAS PROBABLY A PRIESTESS (ARCHAEOLOGICAL MUSEUM, HERAKLION).

2

THE ARCHAIC PERIOD

THE FORMATION OF THE POLIS

The Archaic period is generally divided into "Early Archaic" (730-580) and "Late Archaic" (580-490), but authoritative scholars have set the beginning of the Archaic period toward the year 1000. In order to simplify periodization problems, here we will use the term "Archaic" for the era between the end of the "dark" centuries (9th/8th centuries) and the Persian Wars. From a cultural standpoint, the beginning of the Archaic period is distinguished by the spread of writing and the establishment of the *polis*. The *polis* was a community of people. This term does not identify the material structures of a settlement but the people who populated it, the citizens (*politai*) in an institutional sense. Human settlements, surrounded by defensive walls, existed in the East for thousands of years, but the extraordinary innovation brought about by the *polis* was the libertarian element introduced into the relationship of power between rulers and their subjects. The polis was an "integrated" structure opened to the dialectics of economic interests, social mobility, the exchange of roles and the fundamental rights of people (with the exception of slaves). It is difficult for the modern reader to grasp the formation process of the polis, above all as far as urban planning is concerned. Material documentation is scarce, particularly for the cities of the motherland during the most remote periods. It is somewhat easier to interpret the layout and urban development of the colonies established starting in the 8th century BC. One of the key elements in the establishment of the polis can be found in the relationship between the village and the Archaic city. Following the crisis of the Mycenaean world and the disappearance – or reorganization – of the system composed of the citadel/palace system (*asty*) and the rural district (*damos*), the Greek countryside was dotted with rural communities. The basis of these villages was the *oikos* (house, family), an extended family that included slaves and was intended as a self-sufficient production unit that relied on farming. Trade quickly became the driving force behind this social structure, because bartering farm surpluses represented the only way to obtain whatever the *oikos* did not produce. The economic dynamism generated wealth for some kings (*basileis*) and

heads of the large *oikoi*, accelerating social diversification. Nevertheless, the agricultural space of the community continued to be the starting point for any activity. The polis was formed by merging several villages, through a process the ancients referred to as synoechism (*synoikismòs*, going to live together), in which the common choice of a place of worship played an important role. This encouraged the solidarity of the community around its material aspects (a sacrificial altar and then a temple) as well as its symbolic meaning (ritual). Equally important for the inhabitants was the choice of an open central space where they could meet, exchange goods and participate in governing the community: this was the agora, or meeting place. It is difficult to define the formation process of the polis based on a single model. To cite one of the best-known examples, ancient Sparta always maintained a village organization, but it was consolidated by the powerful symbol of a unifying place of worship, the temple of the tutelary deity (Athena Chalkioikos, "Athena of the Bronze House"), and the agora. Starting in the Early Archaic, Athens acquired a unitary structure around the Acropolis, the seat of the tutelary cult of Athena, and the agora, the seat of the assembly, the council and the magistracies. Participation in community life continued to be governed by a system based on the four ancient tribes (*phylai*) into which the population of Attica was divided. At the end of the 9th century, driven by exceptional population growth (sparked by a full-fledged "agricultural revolution" following the introduction of the plow) the community surpassed the level of the *oikoi* of the Geometric period and was transformed into a unitary structure. It gradually became "monumentalized" in terms of its places of worship and government, whereas games, festivals and rituals helped strengthen the sense of common belonging and solidarity. The entire citizenship was called upon to manage the "common thing" (*koinon*), through executive power exercised initially by the king and then by a magistrate known as an archon, who served for a specific period of time and was subject to the law (*nomos*). Because of all these elements, the *polis* is considered the first state governed by law in Western history.

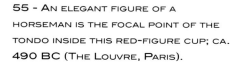

55 - AN ELEGANT FIGURE OF A HORSEMAN IS THE FOCAL POINT OF THE TONDO INSIDE THIS RED-FIGURE CUP; CA. 490 BC (THE LOUVRE, PARIS).

56 - THE SILVER TETRADRACHM FROM ATHENS BEARS THE OWL, THE SYMBOL OF THE CITY, ON THE REVERSE AND THE HEAD OF ATHENA ON THE OBVERSE;

500-490 BC (BRITISH MUSEUM, LONDON).

57 - THE STELE OF "PENSIVE ATHENA", WHICH SHOWS THE GODDESS WEARING A PEPLOS AND HELMET AS SHE LEANS AGAINST A LANCE, IS A SEVERE-STYLE PORTRAIT OF THE PROTECTRESS OF THE ATTIC *POLIS* (ACROPOLIS MUSEUM, ATHENS).

The intensification of trade and colonizing movements contributed decisively to the process of mutual awareness and the acknowledgment of a common identity of the poleis. Panhellenic institutions were established: the Oracle of Apollo at Delphi acquired enormous importance as early as the 8th century. The sanctuary served as a veritable "place of knowledge," as the thousands of pilgrims who went there to ask for the god's advice – important politicians and commoners alike – brought the priests a wealth of information about cities, peoples and lands, near

thetes) was added. Soon the aristocratic state also faced a crisis, triggered by its inability to adapt to new social needs arising from the transformation of the economy during the age of colonization (bringing an increase in crafts and commerce) and the ensuing population growth. One of the key elements in the decline of the aristocracy was the introduction of the phalanx, a battle tactic that set infantrymen in serried ranks. This supplanted the ancient form of warfare in which a handful of warriors, fighting with horses and chariots, decided the outcome of the bat-

and far. This information was then "redistributed" in the form of oracular responses.

Olympia was equally important for the formation of a national conscience. Starting in 776, every four years the youth of Peloponnesus, and then all of Greece, including the islands and colonies, would gather for athletic competitions.

As early as the 8th century, political power was concentrated entirely in the hands of the great aristocratic families, which had ousted the monarchical regime. In some cases, the nobles replaced a hereditary and lifetime monarchy with a temporary one. Toward the mid-8th century Athens was headed by a single archon, who remained in office for 10 years, but starting in 683 or 682 the archonship became annual. Subsequently, a polemarch assisted the king-archon as the commander of the army, and then a college of six judges/legislators (known as thesmo-

tle. The decisive role played by the hoplites in war (the word hoplite comes from hopla, or weapons) added to their importance in peacetime, above all in their rightful claim to participate in managing the koinon. This gradually led to a "politeia of the hoplites," represented by citizens who could afford to outfit themselves, and this transition marked a decisive step toward the democratization of the polis. The codification of law was equally important, particularly with regard to penal law, which took on the delicate area of the reduction to slavery for debts.

Throughout the Archaic period, tension developed in the cities, sometimes leading to open fighting (staseis, rebellion) among social groups for participation in the exercise of power, and to encourage the transition from a type of justice administered by powerful families to state legislation.

58 LEFT - ARISTOCLES SCULPTED THIS CLEARLY OUTLINED BAS-RELIEF FUNERARY STELE FOR THE ATHENIAN HOPLITE ARISTION; 520-510 BC (NATIONAL ARCHAEOLOGICAL MUSEUM, ATHENS).

58 RIGHT - THIS RELIEF FROM THE LATE ARCHAIC PERIOD DEPICTS A FORMATION OF SOLDIERS ON A CHARIOT AND ON FOOT (HOPLITES); CA. 500 BC (NATIONAL ARCHAEOLOGICAL MUSEUM, ATHENS).

59 - THIS BLACK-FIGURE *HYDRIA* PORTRAYS A FIGHT BETWEEN TWO WARRIORS ARMED WITH LANCES. A SOLDIER FELLED IN BATTLE LIES AT THEIR FEET; CA. 560 BC (THE LOUVRE, PARIS).

With very few exceptions, the *poleis* divided their populations into three groups: citizens with full rights, foreigners and slaves. Citizens were distinguished by the fact that they belonged to two social classes, the conservative aristocrats, who were large landowners, and the masses, composed of small farmers and craftsmen.

In Sparta only the Spartiate were citizens. They were "peers" by right (*homoioi*), descendents of the Dorians who had arrived in the Peloponnesus at the end of the 2nd millennium and prevailed over the Achaeans. Because of this privileged position, they could exploit the land without actually working it. Below them in the social stratification were the *perioeci* ("those dwelling around") of Laconia and Messenia, who were free but had no political rights. They worked as traders and artisans, paying part of their income to the city; they were also required to serve in the army. Lastly, the helots were pre-Dorian natives who, subjected and reduced to servility, worked as farmhands.

On a political level, Sparta was ruled by two kings, who commanded the army; a council of elders (*gherusia*) with just 28 members, who had the power to legislate and judge the most serious crimes; and the assembly of the Spartiate (*apella*), responsible for approving laws. A council of five ephors ("those who observe") oversaw the political institutions. This was a rigidly conservative type of government that barred any type of influence from the outside world. In fact, foreigners were not allowed to live in the city, and the Spartiate thus shunned innovation and openness.

The political history of Athens, on the other hand, was characterized by an extremely dynamic society. It developed from a monarchy into an aristocratic land-based oligarchy, a transition that was championed by the archon. The crisis of the aristocratic class in the face of the new entrepreneurial ranks of merchants and craftsmen, who aspired to power, led to Solon's reforms in the early 6th century, thereby drawing the production classes into government. Access to the city magistracies was based on wealth, and the citizens were divided four classes. Those who had an income of at least 500 *medimni* of wheat (1 *medimnus* equals about 1.5 bushels) or *metretes* of oil (1 *metrete* equals about 10 gallons) were known as *pentacosiomedimni*, the *triacosiomedimni* or *hippeis* had between 300 and 500 *medimni* or *metretes*, the *zeugitae* owned a plot of arable land and a pair of oxen (*zeugos*), and the *thetes* owned no property. Only the first two classes could hold the office of archon. The purpose of Solon's reform was to reestablish the ownership of small farms, which had seriously been undermined by extensive debts and thus the loss of freedom. Solon abolished slavery for indebtedness and introduced a type of devaluation that alleviated debts. The most important change, however, was the Heliaia ("people's assembly"), formed by drawing lots among all citizens over the age of 30.

Athenians could petition the Heliaia against the decisions of magistrates, but not those of the Areopagus (the supreme tribunal). From a cultural standpoint, the 7th and 6th centuries were distinguished by the spread of writing and the rise of Archaic lyric poetry.

The Archaic period was one of colonization, with movements toward southern Italy and Sicily, the Mediterranean coasts

60 - The inscription "Solon" or "nomothetes" is carved in the lower section of this classical herm, known as the Bust of Solon. However, some critics think it portrays the tragedian Sophocles; 1st century BC (Uffizi Gallery, Florence).

61 - This herm portrays Pittacus, one of the Seven Sages and a lawmaker from Mytilene, who lived during the 6th century BC; Roman copy after the bronze original from 340-330 BC (The Louvre, Paris).

of modern-day France, the Iberian peninsula, the Black Sea, the Dardanelles and the coasts of North Africa. The colonization process was led mainly by the isthmian cities of Corinth and Megara, the Euboean cities of Chalcis and Eretria, and the Ionian city of Miletus. Several causes sparked this trend: population growth, political tension within the *poleis*, the need for large aristocratic families to avoid splitting up their lands (to prevent the dispersion of property, the entire inheritance went to the eldest son, whose siblings were thus forced to seek their fortunes elsewhere), and the search for new markets. This diaspora around the Mediterranean gave the Greeks strategic positions in trade and relations, which ultimately went beyond purely material interests to involve culture and art.

Starting in the 7th century, the tyrannies brought an element of dynamism to the political, social and cultural transformation of the city. Clashes between groups and factions within a *polis* often led to the rise of great individual power, backed by the most active classes – the entrepreneurs (merchants and craftsmen) – to the detriment of landed aristocracy. The growing ranks of hoplites, or foot soldiers, who were part of the phalanx of the polis, and the strong bond between these men and their leaders, helped the boldest and most capable commanders – who were often members of the aristocracy – rise to power. Several names (Cypselus, Periander, Peisistratus, Polycrates) are tied not only to the political history of the middle and final phases of the Archaic period, but also to the development of Greek culture. In fact, tyranny did not simply mean the violent and unregulated exercise of power: paradoxically, the tyrant's actions encouraged the rise of democracy toward the end of the Archaic period.

THE ART OF THE GEOMETRIC PERIOD

At the beginning of the 8th century, the Greek world was virtually uniform from a cultural standpoint, though it manifested some regional variety. Once again, the richest documentation comes from pottery.

Athens played a predominant role. As far as vase shapes are concerned, the repertory was essentially the same as that of the Protogeometric period. A few figured elements began to appear in the austere geometric fabric: initially horses, boars and small deer, followed by men dueling, land and sea battles, and scenes showing the "display" of the dead. Like Athens, soon Corinth, Argos, Sparta, Euboea, the Cyclades and Crete also developed their own pottery.

During the final phase of the Geometric period in Athens, a class of large funerary vessels became widespread, the most notable of which by the Dipylon Master, the first clearly recognizable artistic personality in Western art history. His workshop produced monumental vases used as funerary markers at the necropolis near the Double Gate or *dipylon*, hence the name. This testifies to a sudden concentration of wealth in the hands of a small social class. Within a rigorously geometric decorative system, the human figure was portrayed according to a model that remained in style until the late 8th century: the head and legs were depicted in profile, the chest – triangular – was portrayed frontally, the arms were slender, and the calves and thighs were exaggerated. Despite its geometric rigidity, this kind of figure could easily be adapted in elaborate and dramatic scenes such as battles, shipwrecks and funerary rituals (which may reflect the historic situation and the ideals of the aristocracy, as also expressed by Homeric poetry).

The first human and animal representations also appeared in sculpture starting at the end of the 9th century. These bronze, ivory and terracotta statues were purely "functional." Forms became better defined and bodies – still devoid of organic unity – were crafted strictly by addition. In the representation of animals such as horses, mannerist effects were achieved through the inconsistent rendering of geometric forms: slender bodies, elongated legs and pointy knees, "flared" faces and plumed manes.

63 CENTER AND RIGHT -
THE LARGE BOEOTIAN BELL
IDOL PRESENTS A COMPLEX
GEOMETRIC DECORATION;
CA. 700 BC (THE LOUVRE,
PARIS).

62 - THIS PYXIS WITH
SEAHORSES ON THE LID IS
PART OF THE LATE
GEOMETRIC PRODUCTION OF
ATHENS AND BEARS THE
TYPICAL REPERTORY OF
GAMMADIA, DIAMONDS AND
ROSETTES; CA. 740 BC
(THE LOUVRE, PARIS).

63 LEFT - THE KRATER, DONE IN
THE GEOMETRIC STYLE, IS FROM
THE NECROPOLIS NEAR THE
DIPYLON IN ATHENS. IT DEPICTS
THE CROWDED SCENE OF THE
DISPLAY AND TRANSPORT OF THE
DECEASED; CA. 750 BC
(NATIONAL ARCHAEOLOGICAL
MUSEUM, ATHENS).

No human activity is more closely tied to the political and social structures of an era than architecture. In this case, it developed in relation to a specific practical need of community living – religious (a ritual) or political (an assembly) – but it quickly acquired a symbolic function that was accompanied by a crystallization of forms. Consider the temple. In the Protogeometric and Geometric periods (10th – 8th century BC), the house (*oikos*) of the deities resembled the residence of the *basileus* or king. In turn, these structures looked like typical rural dwellings made of perishable materials (wood, reeds, raw clay). They had a rectangular or apsed plan with walls surrounded by posts that supported a sloped roof. Several terracotta models provide valuable information about the links between these "rural temples" and dwellings, such as the use of perishable materials (the posts and bundles of reeds can easily be distinguished) and the lack of decoration (in several models, the statue of the god is on the roof).

Between the 8th and 7th centuries, these buildings moved beyond the limitations posed by function and acquired symbolic value, emphasizing the aspect of the visible "image" that inspired "wonder." As aesthetics became more important, durable materials (baked clay, stone and marble) began to be employed. A construction system emphasizing the powers at play in the structure (floors, walls, supports, beams, roofs) was adopted, along with a decorative system: the order (*kosmos*) that distinguished the joints, seams and edges (bases, capitals, friezes, ped-

iments). By the 6th century, regional differentiations arose (Peloponnesus, northwest Greece, Attica, the Aegean islands, Aeolia), in which the various "schools" ultimately standardized the architectural orders (Doric, Ionic and Aeolian). Civic space underwent the same transformation as religious space. In this case, however, the process is more difficult to interpret, due to the paucity of material documentation. A minor sense of "monumentality" prevailed, even for important community structures. Despite the fact that there was a need to allocate space for city assemblies starting with the Archaic period, it seems that these structures were quite basic, with elements such as wooden tiers (*ikria*) and the temporary installations we find depicted on vases. The same held true for religious ceremonies, festivals and games. Extraordinary examples of civic buildings finally developed in the 6th century. These included the *ekklesiasteria*, designed for the city assembly (*ekklesia*), and the *bouleuteria*, buildings in which the council (Boule) would meet, as documented in Siceliot ("Sicilian") cities, and in Agrigentum, Metapontum and Paestum in Magna Graecia. In the Archaic tradition, the urbanist was considered the city founder. In the *Odyssey* (Book VI, 7-10), Nausithous erected city walls, assigned urban lots, built temples and allocated fields. The colonial policy of the High Archaic repeatedly posed the problem of the "new city." The model of the "mythical founder," referred to as the *oikistes*, probably originated from the effective role of these colony "experts," who interacted with politicians.

64 LEFT - THIS TERRACOTTA MODEL FROM PERACHORA IS ONE OF THE OLDEST ONES EVER FOUND: IT SHOWS A TYPICAL *OIKOS* WITH AN ATRIUM, APSED PLAN AND CONVEX ROOF; CA. 750 BC (NATIONAL ARCHAEOLOGICAL MUSEUM, ATHENS).

The 7th century is also known as the Orientalizing Period. Once the geometric balance of forms was overturned, artists discovered the possibility of creating organic images. The inspiration for this extraordinary change came from the East, with its melting pot of cultures.

As far as the artistic sphere is concerned, the Archaic period was characterized by uniform high quality, though there was great differentiation on a local level. This strictly artisanal approach was replaced by a truly artistic one, as demonstrated by the appearance of a large number of signatures proudly placed on finished works.

The Orientalizing period also saw the advent of monumental or "Daedalic" statuary. Daedalus has traditionally been considered the inventor of "living" statues (works well positioned in space and without the primitive stiffness seen in previous eras). These works were characterized by their articulated body structure, sculpted rationally to convey an almost architectural appearance. His oeuvre aspired to ideal beauty, both human and divine, nude (the male figure of the *kouros*) or clothed (the female figure of the *kore*). The image was constructed on parallel planes, and the need to place curved elements such as the eyes and mouth on the frontal plane led to the device of raising the corners of these features. The outcome resembles a smile, the so-called "Archaic smile" of the first modern representations of that art. In the artistic vision of Ionia and the eastern Greece, the planes were reassembled to form a rounded volume (akin to a column), whereas Doric statues maintained a more block-like appearance.

The two leading centers – Athens and Corinth – continued to produce top-quality pottery. In Athens – faithful to its tradition of monumentality – important artists such as the Analatos Painter and the Polyphemus Painter appeared on the scene. They used outlining, color and incised decorations to create magnificent representations and portray mythical episodes in a narrative form. Oriental figurative and ornamental motifs enriched the repertory of local workshops. Corinthian production, rooted in Orientalizing decorativeness (sequences of real animals and monstrous creatures, floral motifs, processions of soldiers, dancers, musicians), became somewhat careless and less refined, and was ultimately surpassed in the late 7th century.

64 RIGHT - ON THIS CLAY TEMPLE MODEL FROM THE HERAION OF ARGOS, THE PAINTED DECORATION DEMONSTRATES THE CARPENTRY METHODS USED FOR CONSTRUCTION; CA. 700 BC (NATIONAL ARCHAEOLOGICAL MUSEUM, ATHENS).

65 - THIS CLOSE-UP OF THE RELIEF AMPHORA FROM THEBES SHOWS PERSEUS SLAYING THE GORGON. THE DECORATION PRESENTS TYPICAL ELEMENTS OF THE ORIENTALIZING STYLE, SUCH AS ANIMAL MOTIFS AND FANCIFUL DECORATIONS; CA. 680 BC (THE LOUVRE, PARIS).

66 - IN THE MID-6TH CENTURY, THE POTTERY PRODUCED IN CORINTH MAINLY DEPICTED CATS, SPHINXES, SIRENS AND GORGON MASKS (BRITISH MUSEUM, LONDON).

67 - THE FEMALE HEAD, MADE OF TERRACOTTA, WAS FROM AN ACROTERIAL FIGURE OF A SPHINX DISCOVERED IN THEBES; 6TH CENTURY BC (THE LOUVRE, PARIS).

68 - THIS *KORE* FROM THE ACROPOLIS
IN ATHENS ILLUSTRATES THE IONIC STYLE
THAT DISTINGUISHED THE CREATIONS OF
THE LATE ARCHAIC PERIOD,
PARTICULARLY IN THE INTRICATE AND
ELEGANT HAIRSTYLE; CA. 525 BC
(ACROPOLIS MUSEUM, ATHENS).

69 - THE FUNERARY STATUE OF THE
ANAVYSSOS *KOUROS* HAS BEEN
ATTRIBUTED TO THE YOUNG CRESUS
FROM THE NOBLE FAMILY OF THE
ALCMEONIDS, FROM WHICH
CLEISTHENES DESCENDED; CA. 530 BC
(NATIONAL ARCHAEOLOGICAL MUSEUM,
ATHENS).

70-71 AND 70 BOTTOM - GYMNASIUM SCENES ARE SCULPTED IN RELIEF ON THE SQUARE BASE OF A *KOUROS* STATUE; 510-500 BC. ONE SIDE OF THE BASE (ABOVE) DEPICTS A GROUP OF EPHEBES PLAYING BALL: NOTE THE EXTREMELY DELICATE PORTRAYAL OF ANATOMIC STRUCTURE OF THE NUDE FIGURE, CREATING A SENSE OF TENSION THAT BORDERS ON THE ABSTRACT (NATIONAL ARCHAEOLOGICAL MUSEUM, ATHENS).

71 BOTTOM - THIS ANIMATED PICTURE OF A CAT AND DOG FIGHTING, WHICH SHOWS WELL-RENDERED FORESHORTENING, DECORATES ANOTHER SIDE OF THE BASE (NATIONAL ARCHAEOLOGICAL MUSEUM, ATHENS).

MATURE ARCHAIC SCULPTURE

The remarkable mobility of artists led to an intense exchange of experiences, above all in sculpture. For example, this type of exchange merged *charis* – Ionic grace – with the solid volumes distinctive of Attic taste. The result was a series of masterpieces such as the *Moschophoros* (ca. 570), the work known as the Rampin Horseman, the *Kore in Dorian Peplos* (ca. 540), and the series of large *korai*, including the Marseille Aphrodite. In all these works, Archaic stiffness was dissolved in simple gestures (bearing gifts, extending offerings, coyly lifting the edge of a gown). Through the substance and solidity of the Attic style, graceful draping, the rippling of lightweight fabrics and the stiffer folds of mantles prevailed over the exteriority and mannerism of the Ionic style.

For the modern scholar, Athens under the tyranny of Peisistratus effectively serves as a remarkable observatory regarding an important aspect of the Greek mentality: the political potential of myth and figurative art in a given historic, economic, social and cultural setting.

For example, the labors of Heracles enjoyed enormous popularity and were often represented on pottery everywhere, including Athens, despite the fact that the hero was not Ionic or Athenian but Doric. However, Athena was also Heracles' protectress, and that fact sufficed. By identifying himself with Heracles, Peisistratus deftly exploited this connection to strengthen his ties with the goddess and the city, and thus justify his power. Numerous Athenian vase paintings of Heracles' ascent to Olympus, accompanied by Athena, clearly reflect the use of this hero for political purposes. This message is evident in Herodotus' account of how Peisistratus managed to return to the city after being exiled temporarily, reaching the Acropolis on a chariot alongside a towering woman dressed like Athena. The pediments of the small sacred buildings erected on the Acropolis during this period also take up this trend, albeit in a more monumental form. They depict the labors of

Heracles, evoked with vibrant figures. The famous pediment of the three-bodied monster is an excellent example.

Monumental grandeur was manifested in the series of pediment statues (of which only fragments remain) sculpted by Antenor at the end of the 6th century for the temple of Apollo at Delphi.

72 - The statue uses solid and rhythmically crafted forms to portray a man carrying a calf on his shoulders (*Moschophoros*). Rhombos dedicated this offering to the Acropolis; ca. 570-560 BC (Acropolis Museum, Athens).

73 - The bearded and crowned head of the Rampin Horseman underscores the noble forms of the Late Archaic, which were still characterized by precious stylized detailing; ca. 550 BC (The Louvre, Paris).

74 - THE ATTIC BLACK-FIGURE CUP BY
EXEKIAS SHOWS DIONYSUS ON A SHIP
WHOSE MAST HAS BEEN TRANSFORMED
INTO A VINE LADEN WITH GRAPE
CLUSTERS. THE DESIGN IS FLUID AND
SOPHISTICATED; 550-540 BC
(STAATLICHE ANTIKENSAMMLUNGEN UND
GLYPTOTHEK, MUNICH).

75 LEFT - THIS BLACK-FIGURE CUP HAS
BEEN ATTRIBUTED TO PAINTER N, A
LITTLE-KNOWN MASTER AT THE
WORKSHOP OF NIKOSTHENES, WHO
"INVENTED" NUMEROUS POTTERY
FORMS; 540-520 BC (STAATLICHE
ANTIKENSAMMLUNGEN UND
GLYPTOTHEK, MUNICH).

75 RIGHT - THE FAMOUS FRANÇOIS
KRATER, THE MASTERPIECE OF THE POTTER
ERGOTIMOS AND THE VASE PAINTER
KLEITIAS, DEPICTS AN ARRAY OF MYTHS.
THIS ATHENIAN WORK REFLECTS THE
INFLUENCE OF COMPETING CORINTHIAN
POTTERY; 570 BC (NATIONAL
ARCHAEOLOGICAL MUSEUM, FLORENCE).

In the field of vase painting, the great Proto-Attic production of the early 7th century prevailed over the Corinthian production, as we have noted. It gradually became less monumental in character, thanks not only to the improvement of vase shapes but also the perfection of narrative language, which turned to the clear composition, syntactical order and stylized detailing distinctive of Corinthian pottery. The masterpiece of this period is a vessel painted by Kleitias for the potter Ergotimos. This work, known as the François krater, recounts several myths, including the dance of Theseus and Ariadne with Athenian children after the Minotaur was slain, the wedding of Peleus and Thetis, and Achilles' ambush of Troilus. Attic artists, who by this time had mastered all technical and expressive media, transferred the solid structure of sculpture to pottery, with lively and exquisitely rendered narratives distinguished by their grace and elegance, using what is known as the black-figure style. Between 550 and 530, vase painters such as Nearchos, Lydos and the Amasis Painter transformed the Archaic language into a more fluid and decorative means of expression. In the dramatic scenes that are the hallmark of his vases (such as the famous Chiusi amphora, now in Berlin, depicting Ajax carrying Achilles' body), Exekias (530) achieved austere dignity and epic grandeur.

Toward 530, the shop of the potter Andokides began to use a new technique. Instead of painting black figures on the reddish surface of the clay, the procedure was reversed, leaving the figures in red and painting the rest of the field black. This made it possible to define the internal details with dense, fluid or fine brushstrokes, as opposed to the incised lines used with the black-figure technique. This method thus moved toward decidedly more pictorial effects that suggested three-dimensional rather than sketched figures. Douris, Onesimos, the Kleophrades Painter and the Berlin Painter are among the masters who worked between the late 6th and early 5th centuries. Euphronios and Euthymides painted large vases with rigorously articulated scenes that convey calm solemnity within monumental spatiality. Well aware of the great artistry expressed by these creations, Euthymides added an eloquent inscription to one of his amphorae, mocking his rival: "Not even Euphronios this"!

76 LEFT - EPIKTETOS LOVED TO PAINT THE INTERNAL TONDO OF CUPS WITH INDIVIDUAL FIGURES, SUCH AS THIS NIMBLE ORIENTAL ARCHER; CA. 520 BC (BRITISH MUSEUM, LONDON).

76 RIGHT - THE HALLMARK OF THE BERLIN PAINTER AND HIS CIRCLE INVOLVED ISOLATING HIS SHARPLY OUTLINED FIGURES — PAINTED WITH EXQUISITE BALANCE — AGAINST THE BLACK GROUND OF THE VASE; 490 BC (BRITISH MUSEUM, LONDON).

77 - THIS LACONIAN BLACK-FIGURE CUP SHOWS CADMUS SLAYING THE DRAGON NEAR A FOUNTAIN; MID-6TH CENTURY BC (THE LOUVRE, PARIS).

THE TEMPLE

As we have noted, the formal and artistic development of the temple went hand in hand with the concept of its endurance, which was essential to give it an ideal and emblematic value above and beyond purely practical purposes. Various experimental paths thus evolved, and by the mid-6th century they led to the harmonious standardized forms known as the Doric and Ionic orders (the Corinthian did not develop until much later).

Rivalry among the *poleis*, the tyrants' aspiration for prestige and approval, the affirmation of Greek culture and power in the colonies, and the desire to enhance the importance of the great Panhellenic sanctuaries were the underlying reasons for the architectural efflorescence of the Late Archaic. Moreover, science was making

great advances during this period at Miletus and in Ionia in general: the application of arithmetic and geometry with Thales; the work of Miletus' philosophers Anaximander and Anaximenes, considered the founders of the experimental method, science and the use of technology; and the work of Hecataeus of Miletus, Pythagoras of Samos and Alcmaeon of Croton.

The literary tradition has also indicated Corinth's fundamental role in the development of Doric architecture. To an even greater extent than the temple of Apollo (ca. 540), the older temple of Artemis (580) at the colony of Corcyra (Corfu) represents the first harmonious fusion in terms of structure (a well-defined rapport between the colonnade and the cella; the rhythm and proportions of the columns and of the metope and triglyphs on the frieze) and decoration (the relief of the Gorgon on the pediment).

Instead, the temple of Hera at Samos (570-60) and the one dedicated to Artemis at Ephesus (560-50) are considered the greatest creations of the Archaic Ionic style. With these edifices, monumentality seems to transcend the human scale: in fact, the ancients considered the Artemision at Ephesus one of the seven wonders of the world. Measuring 180 × 377 ft (54.8 × 115 m), it was surrounded by a double set of 8 × 21 columns (the bottom drums of 36 of the columns were sculpted with processional figures); the cella had an open roof.

THE FOUNDATION OF DEMOCRACY AND THE PERSIAN PERIOD

The laws enacted by the Athenian Solon in 594-93 represented the first important step toward a form of democratic constitution in Greece. Likewise, it was in Athens that, after Hippias, the son of the tyrant Peisistratus, was driven out in 510 with Sparta's aid, Cleisthenes passed fundamental institutional reforms in favor of the people. Elected archon in 508, he divided Attica into ten tribes on a territorial basis, reorganizing the four ancient tribes composed of powerful families and clans. In turn, each tribe was divided into three districts or *trittyes* (one in the valley, one on the coast and one in the hills) as a way to break up or at least minimize particular family ties and economic interests, in order to promote the general ones of the *polis*. Cleisthenes' reform valorized and specified the previous division of Attica into quarters and districts (*demoi*), which rose to over 100 units. Each citizen was enrolled in the *deme* in which he lived, and subsequently he would be identified in documents by the name of the *deme* rather than with his father's name, clearly reflecting a transition from an "aristocratic" name (at least for those who were aristocrats) to a community one. Each tribe would draw lots to choose 50 members of the council (Boule). The council's term of office was one year, and it was headed on a rotating basis for 1/10 of the year by 10 groups of 50 *prytaneis*, who held executive or ruling power. The task of the council as a whole was to set guidelines for domestic and foreign policy, which were then discussed and voted on by the people's assembly (*ekklesia*), which thus regained power with respect to the aristocratic council of the Areopagus. In essence Cleisthenes sought to get all citizens with full rights involved in managing public affairs (though these citizens actually represented a small minority of the population, which was also composed of women, foreigners and slaves), while also trying to weaken "pressure groups," akin to modern-day lobbies.

In the political scenario that characterized the transition from the 6th to the 5th century, the "Persian question" also played a key role. With the conquest of Lydia in the middle of the 6th century, the expansionist drive of the Persian king, Cyrus the Great (ca. 580-529), into Asia Minor put an end to the autonomy of the Greek cities on the Asiatic coast. The subsequent conquest of Egypt (525), Thrace and Macedonia (513-12) by Darius I (550-486) seriously worsened the situation from both a political and economic standpoint. In fact, Lydia had always acted as a sort of protectorate for the Greek *poleis* of Asia, promoting economic prosperity. Instead, the Persians exerted far heavier control, also through the presence of tyrants loyal to the Great King, and they ended up damaging Greek trade in that part of the Mediterranean. Growing discontent flared into open rebellion in 500, first at Miletus and then in the other Ionian cities. The lack of help from the motherland (Athens and Eretria alone sent a few ships) and the massive Persian reaction quickly put an end to the uprising in 494, when Miletus was captured and then destroyed. The Greeks were outraged. More importantly, however, they became acutely aware of the danger the Persians posed to the mainland, galvanizing Athens and Sparta into stipulating a military agreement.

80 - THIS EXQUISITE RELIEF FROM MARATHON PORTRAYS A NUDE HOPLITE, IN THE ARCHAIC KNEELING-RUNNING ATTITUDE, WEARING AN ATTIC HELMET; CA. 500 BC (NATIONAL ARCHAEOLOGICAL MUSEUM, ATHENS).

As for the Persians, their precarious political hold limited to Ionia, which was not far from an area – continental Greece – with a deeply rooted ethos of liberty, inspired their decision to go to the very heart of the matter. With the goal of punishing Athens and Eretria, in 490 a large Persian fleet set sail for the continent, conquering the Cyclades and landing in Euboea. After destroying Eretria, the land troops invaded Attica. At Marathon, however, the Athenian strategist Miltiades used hoplite tactics and, with the help of a small Plataean contingent (the Spartan forces did not arrive until the battle was over), he managed to defeat the much larger Persian army led by Datis and Ataphernes, who had accompanied Hippias, the son of Peisistratus, in attempt to restore him as tyrant of Athens. The importance of the victory, which went well beyond the military sphere, was celebrated in Athens with a funerary monument honoring the fallen – just 200 – and the memory of this battle was destined to endure.

The years that followed saw the overall reinforcement of democratic institutions and social structures. The importance of the policies promoted by Themistocles, who wanted to turn Athens into a maritime trade empire, was decisive. He gave the city a large fleet (which could also be used for defensive purposes), manned by *thetes*, or those who owned no property, who thus acquired political importance as they began to participate in the material management of the city.

When the Persian king Xerxes (519-456) decided to avenge his father Darius in 480 and conquer Greece, defense seemed difficult but not impossible. As soon as they heard about the Persians' massive mobilization, the *poleis* reached an agreement and formed a common front, though with a few defections. A formation of 4000 Peloponnesian hoplites, led by the Spartan Leonidas, was sent to Thermopylae, the gateway to central Greece, while the Athenian fleet waited at Cape Artemisius, in Euboea. Though the Persians broke through at Thermopylae (where Leonidas' 300 heroic Spartans were killed) and captured Athens, the great Greek naval victory at Salamis marked Persia's defeat, confirmed the following year (479) by the Greeks' victory in the Battle of Plataea and the definitive triumph of Hellenic liberty over Oriental despotism.

81 - THE STRATEGIST TYPE OF BUST, WITH AN ATTIC HELMET, IS TRADITIONALLY THOUGHT TO PORTRAY THEMISTOCLES, THOUGH SOME CRITICS HAVE DISPUTED THIS; COPY FROM THE ROMAN PERIOD (NATIONAL ARCHAEOLOGICAL MUSEUM, NAPLES).

3

THE CLASSICAL PERIOD

The Persian conflict formally came to an end in 449 when, following a last victorious battle at Cyprus, Athens signed a peace treaty – known as the Peace of Callias, after the ambassador who negotiated it – affirming the city's domination of the Aegean. In addition to this military leadership, Pericles also strived to promote Athens' political, economic and cultural supremacy. This led to the "miracle" of Periclean Athens, but to understand it we must backtrack and consider all the historical conditions that made it possible.

Following the dramatic events that occurred between 490 and 479 Athens and Sparta, victorious over the Persians but already competing for supremacy over Greece, reinforced their individual power: the Lacedaemonians on land and the Athenians at sea. In 478 Athens founded the Delian or Delian-Attic League, a confederation that united numerous cities and islands of the Aegean under the city's leadership, opposing the Peloponnesian League founded earlier by Sparta. The declared

purpose of the Delian-Attic League was to keep the Persian threat in check. In reality, however, it catered to the great *polis'* imperialistic aims with respect to its allies, which were forced to pay a tax to maintain the fleet and allow ten Athenian magistrates to administer the treasury of the League, which was kept in Delos until 454 but was then moved to Athens.

In Sparta the two most important powers of the state clashed: the kings, who were more open to a quasi-democratic discussion of domestic polity, and the ephors, the severe defenders of conservatism. In the meantime, Athens took a series of steps designed to consolidate political, economic and commercial expansion. Initially, government jobs were created, such as the people's courts (*dikasteria*) and the cleruchies (*klerouchiai*), colonial bodies established to monitor the allies. Major public works were then undertaken, notably the Long Walls that extended as far as Piraeus. All these initiatives tied the urban masses to the management of state interests. The powerful tension between Cimon's conservative party and the more innovative one headed by Themistocles, and — within the latter — the dissension caused by the radical democratic wing of Ephialtes, were quelled with Pericles' rise to the position of strategos, as he ushered in the triumph of democracy.

The style that distinguishes the art of the period between the Persian Wars and the Age of Pericles has been referred to as "severe" by modern critics, due to its divergence from the hallmark of Archaic art: the distinctive "smile" of human and divine figures.

Direct and "visual" knowledge of the art of the Severe period is quite fragmentary, but literary and epigraphic sources provide extensive information about artists and works.

In sculpture, the migration of Ionian artists following the "Persian question" led to the establishment of numerous workshops on the Greek continent, above all in Athens. Public commissions developed alongside private ones: following the rousing victory over the Persians and due also to rivalries with other *poleis*, each city dedicated votive offerings (*anathemata*), with the clear intention of affirming their prestige, above all in the Panhellenic sanctuaries. The great sculptures of the era were made of bronze: at Argos with Ageladas; Aegina with Onatas; Sicyon with Kanachos; Athens with Kritios, Hegias and Hegesias; and Rhegion, in southern Italy, with Pythagoras. Alongside abundant small-scale sculptures (such as figured bronzes, tripods and mirrors), several works by the great masters have also come down to us through marble copies, such as the famous group of the Athenian *Tyrannicides* (Harmodius and Aristogeiton) sculpted by Kritios and Nesiotes, *Apollo Sitting on the Omphalos* and *Aphrodite Sosandra* by Kalamis, Myron's *Discobolus (Discus Thrower)* and the group of *Athena and Marsyas*. However, there are also several bronze masterpieces whose authorship scholars have yet to determine: the *Charioteer* from Delphi, the *Zeus/Poseidon* from Cape Artemision, and other marble works such as the pediment statues from the Temple of Zeus at Olympia.

G. Becatti, a renowned historian of ancient art, wrote that the vigorous and turgid volumes of the Severe style seem to interpret the heroic conception of life typical of the generation that experienced the Persian Wars. The bodies are robust, rounded and natural, and the excessive attention to intricate and highly decorative detailing distinctive of the Archaic vision was abandoned in favor of more organically articulated volume. The *Kritios Boy* at the Acropolis in Athens can be considered the manifesto of this style: the head, slightly turned, breaks away from the frontality of the Archaic figure, and a new sense of weight and rhythm gives the entire body greater spatial balance. An even freer interpretation of this theme is evident in *Apollo Alexikakos* ("restrainer of evil"), also known as *Apollo Sitting on the Omphalos*, by Kalamis. Dynamism and energy burst onto the artistic scene with the *Tyrannicides*. Instead, restrained grace is expressed by the face of *Aphrodite Sosandra*, "saver of men," whose composure, elegance and serenity are eloquently expressed by the mantle that envelops her and, with a few heavy folds, lends movement to the body structure beneath. The bronze original of the *Charioteer* at Delphi has been attributed to the Peloponnesian area. This work shows architectural simplicity in the garments and an intensely dynamic sense of volume in the limbs and head, though a trace of the stylized detailing of the Archaic remains (evident above all in the hair). The artwork of Attica is reflected by the extraordinary sculptor Myron, who probed the composition of sculptural rhythm: his *Discobolus* captures the athlete as he is about the hurl the discus. The figure, taut and concentrated in the broad semicircle of his arms, is balanced by the *contrapposto* curve of his powerful torso.

82 - THE FRAGMENT IS FROM A VOTIVE RELIEF TONDO WITH THE HEAD OF A DEITY — POSSIBLY APHRODITE — FROM MILOS; CA. 460 BC (NATIONAL ARCHAEOLOGICAL MUSEUM, ATHENS).

84 left - THE STATUE OF AN EPHEBE, ATTRIBUTED TO KRITIOS, POWERFULLY REFLECTS THE ATHLETIC IDEAL THAT DOMINATED THE ART OF THE SEVERE PERIOD; CA. 480 BC (ACROPOLIS MUSEUM, ATHENS).

84 right - THE GROUP OF *THE TYRANNICIDES* (HARMODIUS AND ARISTOGEITON) WAS SCULPTED BY KRITIOS AND NESIOTES IN 477-76 BC (NATIONAL ARCHAEOLOGICAL MUSEUM, NAPLES).

86 left -
The bronze statue of
Poseidon (or Zeus,
according to some
scholars) from Cape
Artemision in Euboea was a
treasury commemorating
the victory over the
Persians; 470-460 BC
(National Archaeological
Museum, Athens).

86 right - Myron's
Discobolus (Discus
Thrower) is
unquestionably one of the
most famous works from
the Classical period: it
captures all the tension
of the athlete as he is
about the hurl the discus;
ca. 450 BC (Vatican
Museums, Vatican City).

87 - THE FAMOUS
CHARIOTEER OF DELPHI WAS
COMMISSIONED BY
POLYZALOS, THE TYRANT OF
GELA, TO CELEBRATE
VICTORY IN THE CHARIOT
RACE AT DELPHI; CA. 475
BC (DELPHI MUSEUM).

Critics agree that the pinnacle of this art was achieved with the statues decorating the pediments of the Temple of Zeus at Olympia, sculpted by an anonymous master in about 460, along with the reliefs of the metopes (with *The Labors of Heracles*). The complex of the two pediments celebrated local myths, portraying preparations for the chariot race, held before Zeus, between young Pelops and King Oenomaus for the hand of the king's daughter Hippodamia (east pediment), and the battle between Theseus and Peirithoös, helped by Apollo, against the Centaurs (west pediment). The solid and organic vitality of the nudes is balanced by the dense physicality of the draping. The forms are powerfully alive, yet show a simple vision in which detailing is effaced in favor of overall unity. The only difference between the two series of works is the static aura – solemn and isolating – of the sculptures facing east with respect to the agitated, complex and even turbulent composition of the opposite side. In both cases, this marks the first time that we find decisive characterization of the faces. Nevertheless, the search for expressiveness is limited to defining types and psychological situations rather than individuals (the young man, the old man, pain, dignity). The portraits from the first half of the 5th century also convey types rather than individual features. For example, the Themistocles herm portrays an archetypal *strategos*, with a beard, furrowed brow and helmet.

88 TOP - THE WEST PEDIMENT OF THE TEMPLE OF ZEUS CONVEYS ALL THE SUSPENSE OF THE RACE BETWEEN PELOPS AND KING OENOMAUS, WHEREAS THE WEST PEDIMENT PORTRAYS THE TENSE AND VIOLENT BATTLE BETWEEN THESEUS AND PEIRITHOÖS – HELPED BY APOLLO – AGAINST THE CENTAURS, WHICH HAD KIDNAPPED THE LAPITHAE; CA. 460 BC (OLYMPIA MUSEUM).

88 bottom - The close-up of one of the 12 sculpted metopes from the Temple of Zeus at Olympia illustrates one of the labors of Heracles, the slaying of the Cretan bull; ca. 460 BC (Olympia Museum).

89 - The old soothsayer is clearly concerned about the outcome of the race between the king and Hippodamia's young suitor (Olympia Museum).

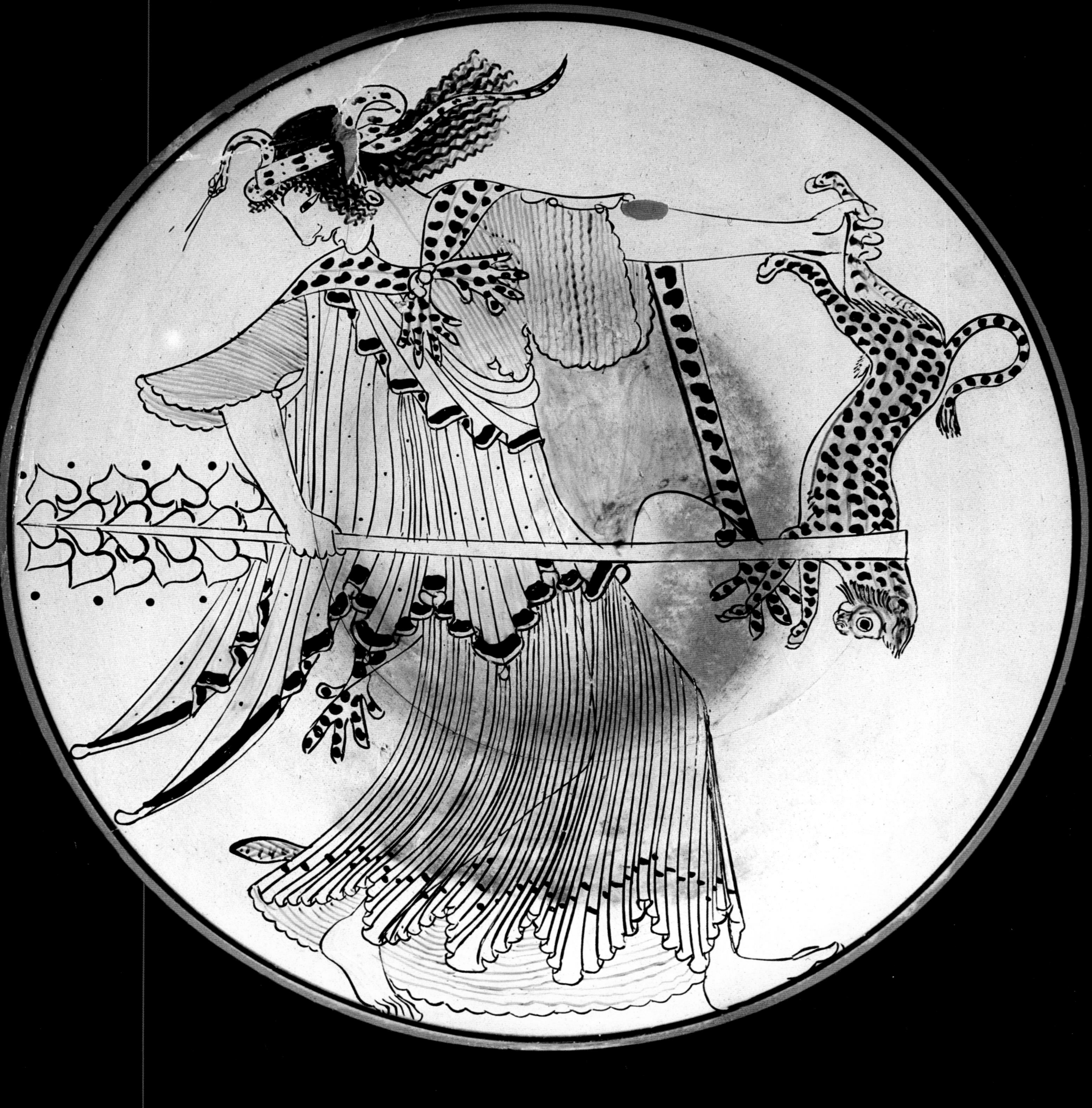

In painting, full mastery of foreshortening was accompanied by the introduction of chiaroscuro, with the skillful use of diluted paint. Consequently, on vases we can glimpse traces of the great art of painting, described by the ancients, which had been lost. In particular, we find the expression of ethos, sentiment, and the intimate essence of the individual and the soul. The champion of this style was Polygnotus. In large frescoes at Delphi and Athens, he expressed his figures' mood not only through the theme of the myth being represented, but also with the displacement of these figures in space, and through their gestures and bearing (the study of facial expression would come later). The pottery masterpieces of the Penthesilea Painter, Polygnotus, the Boreas Painter and the Niobid Painter beautifully interpret these concepts and demonstrate the attempt to overcome the sketched and stylized limitations of vase painting to strive for depth, the organization of space (*skenographia*), and the use of color, light and shadows (*skiagraphia*) inherent in large-scale paintings.

91 RIGHT - THE TONDO IN THIS ATTIC RED-FIGURE KYLIX DEPICTS THESEUS SLAYING THE MINOTAUR. THE OUTSIDE BORDER REPRESENTS OTHER EPISODES FROM THE LIFE OF THE HERO; 440-430 BC (BRITISH MUSEUM, LONDON).

90 - ON THIS *KYLIX*, THE BRYGOS PAINTER CREATED A GRACEFUL MAENAD WITH A PANTHER, AN ANIMAL SACRED TO DIONYSUS; CA. 490 BC (STAATLICHE ANTIKENSAMMLUNGEN UND GLYPTOTHEK, MUNICH).

91 LEFT - SKYTHES PAINTED THIS GROOMING SCENE ON THE GROUND OF THIS RED-FIGURE *KYLIX*; MADE IN THE LATE 6TH CENTURY BC (THE LOUVRE, PARIS).

92 RIGHT - THE *HYDRIA* OF THE MEIDIAS PAINTER PORTRAYS *THE RAPE OF THE DAUGHTERS OF LEUCIPPUS* IN THE UPPER REGISTER OF THE DECORATION AND *HERACLES IN THE GARDEN OF THE HESPERIDES* IN THE LOWER ONE; 410 BC (BRITISH MUSEUM, LONDON).

93 - THE CALYX KRATER ATTRIBUTED TO THE NIOBID PAINTER PORTRAYS *THE CREATION OF PANDORA* IN THE UPPER REGISTER OF THE DECORATION AND A SATYRIC CHORUS IN THE LOWER ONE; 470-460 BC (BRITISH MUSEUM, LONDON).

92 LEFT - THIS BLACK-FIGURE LEKYTHOS DEPICTS OEDIPUS CHALLENGING THE SPHINX; EARLY 5TH CENTURY BC (THE LOUVRE, PARIS).

92 CENTER - THE CALYX KRATER ATTRIBUTED TO THE WORKSHOP OF THE POTTER AISON PORTRAYS THE GIGANTOMACHY; CA. 440 BC (NATIONAL ARCHAEOLOGICAL MUSEUM, FERRARA).

Temple architecture elegantly expresses the period's transition from the pomp of the Archaic to the rigor of the Classical period. The Temple of Athena Aphaia at Aegina achieved – on a small scale – an exquisite balance between agility and the dense rhythm of the columns, not only in the outside ring of the peristasis but also in the fast-paced chiaroscuro of the aisles in the cella. The sculptural decoration of the pediments also openly states the transition from the Archaic ideal to the new "severe" arrangement of volumes.

The vigorous and powerful proportions typical of the aesthetics of the artistic centers of the Peloponnesus becomes more subdued in the Temple of Zeus built at Olympia by the architect Libon, who used more harmonic modular principles. Here we also find the first attempts at optical correction, intended to permit more balanced appreciation of the building as a whole when viewed from a distance. The building yards of the great temples of Sicily and Magna Graecia (Selinus, Agrigentum, Syracuse and Poseidonia/Paestum) represented important fields of experimentation for this research.

During this period, "dialectal" forms and trends typical of local and regional architecture disappeared, and there was a move toward rhythm and symmetry, the balance between parts and volumes, and decorative simplicity, aspects that subsequently became the guiding principles of Classical architecture.

A focus on rationality also became the predominant theme in urban planning, and an important school of thought developed at Miletus.

94-95 - THIS FIGURE OF A FALLEN SOLDIER IS FROM THE EAST PEDIMENT OF THE TEMPLE OF APHAIA AT AEGINA, AND IT MARKS THE TRANSITION FROM THE ARCHAIC VISION OF THE HUMAN FIGURE TO THE SEVERE STYLE; 490-480 BC (STAATLICHE ANTIKENSAMMLUNGEN UND GLYPTOTHEK, MUNICH).

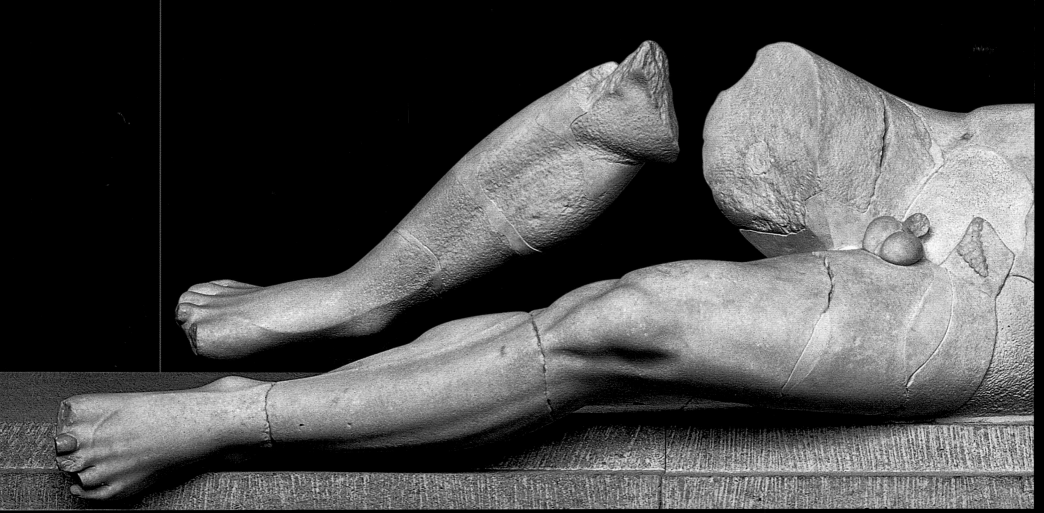

96 - THE CULT OF ATHENA MERGED WITH THAT OF APHAIA ("THE ONE WHO DISAPPEARED"), A CRETAN GODDESS WHO PLUNGED INTO THE SEA TO ESCAPE MINOS, WHO HAD FALLEN IN LOVE WITH HER (STAATLICHE ANTIKENSAMMLUNGEN UND GLYPTOTHEK, MUNICH).

97 TOP RIGHT - THE PEDIMENTS OF THE TEMPLE AT AEGINA ILLUSTRATE THE FIRST AND SECOND EXPEDITIONS AGAINST TROY, IN WHICH AEGINIAN HEROES PARTICIPATED.

97 BOTTOM - THE FIGURE OF ATHENA STANDS OUT IN THE MIDDLE OF THE WEST PEDIMENT OF THE TEMPLE AT AEGINA. AJAX TELAMONIUS AND A TROJAN WARRIOR ARE NEXT TO HER; 500-490 BC (STAATLICHE ANTIKENSAMMLUNGEN UND GLYPTOTHEK, MUNICH).

97 TOP LEFT - THE TEMPLE OF ATHENA APHAIA IS A DORIC BUILDING WITH 6x12 COLUMNS, A CELLA DIVIDED INTO THREE AISLES, A *PRONAOS* AND AN *OPISTHODOMOS* WITH TWO COLUMNS BETWEEN THE PARTITIONS; CA. 510 BC.

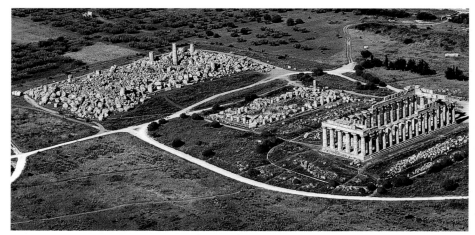

98 TOP - ON THE HILL OF MARINELLA DI SELINUNTE (GREEK SELINUS), THE REMAINS OF TEMPLES E, F AND G TESTIFY TO THE STRICT MODULAR ARRANGEMENT OF THE PLAN AND ELEVATION.

98 CENTER AND 98-99 - AT TEMPLE E, WE FIND A COMPLEX SYSTEM OF OPTICAL CORRECTION AND PROPORTIONAL RATIOS, MAKING IT AN EXCELLENT EXAMPLE OF THE HARMONY DISTINCTIVE OF THE EARLY CLASSICAL PERIOD.

98 BOTTOM - THE METOPES FROM TEMPLE E AT SELINUS REVEAL DEPENDENCE ON GREEK MODELS AS FAR AS MYTHOLOGICAL THEMES ARE CONCERNED, BUT ADHERENCE TO LOCAL TASTE IN THE ARCHAIZING OF THE DRAPERY AND THE POWERFUL EXPRESSIVE ACCENTS. THIS IS EVIDENT IN THE FIGURE OF HERACLES GRASPING THE AMAZON'S CAP (LEFT), THE ANIMATED DOGS TEARING ACTAEON TO PIECES (CENTER) AND THE MARBLE INSERTS OF THE FACES OF THE FIGURES IN THE SCENE PORTRAYING THE MARRIAGE OF ZEUS AND HERA (REGIONAL ARCHAEOLOGICAL MUSEUM, PALERMO).

100 and 101 - The metopes from Temple C on the Selinus acropolis show an anachronistic language that uses the squat and heavy modules typical of the Archaic period; 2nd half of the 6th century BC (Regional Archaeological Museum, Palermo).

102 TOP - THE TEMPLE OF JUNO AT THE SOUTHEAST EDGE OF THE HILL OF THE TEMPLES OF AGRIGENTUM IS A DORIC STRUCTURE BUILT IN THE 5TH CENTURY BC.

102 BOTTOM LEFT - THE TEMPLE OF THE DIOSCURI AT AGRIGENTUM IS ACTUALLY A PICTURESQUE "RUIN" BUILT IN THE 19TH CENTURY USING ELEMENTS FROM DIFFERENT PERIODS FOUND NEAR A DORIC TEMPLE FROM THE MID-5TH CENTURY BC.

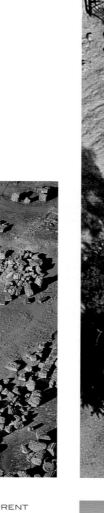

102 BOTTOM RIGHT - THE CURRENT APPEARANCE OF THE TEMPLE OF JUNO IS THE OUTCOME OF RESTORATION AND RECONSTRUCTION WORK THAT BEGAN IN THE 1700S.

102-103 - THE HARMONIOUS STRUCTURE OF THE TEMPLE OF CONCORD AT AGRIGENTUM WAS PRESERVED AS A RESULT OF ITS TRANSFORMATION INTO A CHRISTIAN CHURCH; CA. 440 BC.

CA. 500 BC.

Pericles' policies unquestionably encouraged widespread participation of the masses in governing Athens, because the payment of a daily "allowance" allowed all citizens, even the less well-to-do, to hold public office. Access to the archonship was open to the third income class, the *zeugitae*. The custom of drawing lots was extended to nearly all the magistracies, with the exception of those requiring specific technical and military skills (*strategoi*). Nevertheless, Athens was a democracy limited to a small part of society: full citizens and the sons of Athenians, thereby excluding foreign residents, referred to as *metics*, as well as slaves and all women. In reality, Pericles himself tended to go outside these bounds, personally deciding what was in the common interest and what was best for the state. In short, despite these principles, there seemed to be a streak of totalitarianism.

"So, in what was nominally a democracy, power was really in the hands of the first citizen": Thucydides' words eloquently convey the full problem of this situation and the figure involved. D. Musti, an historian of Ancient Greece, has suggested that the main characteristic of Greek democracy lies in the attempt to harmonize private and public, to coordinate the former with respect to the latter, but without subordinating it. In his most famous discourse, the eulogy for the men slain at Marathon, Pericles affirmed, "Our public men have, besides politics, their private affairs to attend to, and our ordinary citizens, though occupied with the pursuits of industry, are still fair judges of public matters" (Thucydides, *The History of the Peloponnesian War*, Book II, 36 ff). This reflects a rapport between public and private that, due to the confusion of the two spheres, is a controversial issue in politics even today. The Greek historiographic texts that have been handed down to us have shown little interest in the issue of the rules of democracy and the way it worked or, in other words, its process. It is taken for granted that in a democracy the involvement of citizens is sufficient to guarantee the legitimacy of the actions to be undertaken. Therefore, what prevailed was the substance of democracy rather than its decision-making methods, and for Pericles the substance was represented by the common interest, freedom and equality before the law.

In foreign policy, in addition to the anti-Persian line already supported by Cimon, Pericles favored and supported opposing Sparta in its ambitious attempt to control all of Greece. This makes it easy to understand why he backed the helots of Messenia, who had struggled against Spartan oppression for centuries.

After stipulating an agreement with Persia (449), Athens signed a thirty-year truce with Sparta and devoted itself to exploiting the Delian-Attic League entirely for its imperialistic goals. To achieve this end, a strong economic base had already been created by exploiting the silver mines of Cape Sounion. This made it possible to mint coins that were "lighter" than gold ones and could thus circulate more easily: the Athenian "owls." The transfer of the League's treasury to the Acropolis (454) further reinforced the economy, essentially providing ready capital even for projects that had not been established in the agreement. After calling all Greeks to a meeting in Athens "to consult and advise concerning the Greek temples which the barbarians had burnt down" – a meeting that never took place due to Spartan opposition – Pericles defied powerful internal opposition to pursue his own ideas. In 450-449, he submitted a proposal to the people's assembly suggesting that the League treasury be used to reconstruct the temples of the Acropolis as a sign of Athens' supremacy. Following heated discussions, his opponents agreed.

106 - THIS PORTRAIT OF PERICLES IS A ROMAN COPY OF THE STATUE SCULPTED BY KRESILAS FOR THE ACROPOLIS IN ATHENS IN ABOUT 440-430 BC (STAATLICHE MUSEEN, BERLIN).

107 - THE ORIGINAL (1ST HALF OF THE 4TH CENTURY BC) OF THIS COPY OF THE STATUE OF ATHENA, FOUND IN CRETE, HAS BEEN ATTRIBUTED TO CEPHISODOTUS, THE FATHER OF PRAXITELES (THE LOUVRE, PARIS).

Though his name is not listed in any official document, Pericles was indeed responsible (*epistates*) for the work that was completed just over a decade later: ancient sources cite this as "Pericles' works" (Plutarch, *Pericles*, 13). This building activity is attributable to a program that revolved around the Acropolis, where the colossal simulacrum of Athena Parthenos ("Virgin"), made of gold and ivory, was created, along with the temple to house it (the *Parthenon* was actually the name of the room behind the cella, so called after the virgins who wove the goddess' mantle, but the name was then extended to the entire building). The Propylaea, or monumental entrance to the clearing of the Acropolis, and the Odeon near its southern slopes, where spectacles connected with the festivities were held, were also built as part of this work.

Other important initiatives can also be credited to Pericles, at least in part, such as construction of a number of marble temples in Attica. However, it is likely that others can be attributed to the Cimonian opposition, such as the Temple of Athena Nike ("Victory") near the entrance to the Acropolis and the large Temple of Hephaestus in the Agora, which were completed after Pericles' death. The Agora was gradually embellished with buildings representing Athens' political sphere, such as the *bouleuterion*, or the meeting place of the assembly (*Boule*), the Temple of Apollo Patroos, the father and protector of the Ionian people, the Stoa of Zeus Eleutherios ("Liberator") with the altar of Zeus Agoraios, the Stoa Basileios or "Royal Stoa" in which laws were displayed, the enclosure of the court of the Heliaia and much more. Cimon's family did extensive work on the public square, building the Tholos for the Prytaneis and the Stoa Poikile or "Painted Stoa," so named because of its famous paintings (in the late 4th century it became the center of the famous school of philosophy

that thus came to be known as Stoicism). This strategic area for the life of the city was left out of Pericles' plans, which concentrated mainly on the Acropolis. The historian L. Beschi has aptly suggested that the bronze statue of Athena Promachos ("Fighter"), completed a few years before the statue of Athena Parthenos, represents the starting point for this entire program. The "armed" Athena, dedicated as a votive offering in about 455-450, was erected in the open space of the Acropolis, which had been left barren following the Persians' destruction of the Archaic temples. In fact, the position of the statue determined the alignment of the new monumental Propylaea and marked an important point in the approach to the Parthenon. The area in front of it was the best point from which to observe this splendid structure in all three dimensions. Phidias was the executor as well as the superintendent (*episkopos*) of the entire Periclean program, and he relied on the assistance of the architects Ictinus and Callicrates.

According to scholars, work began in 448-447, when the base of an old temple, which was never completed due to the Persian invasion, was used to create a new building made entirely of Pentelic marble. It had a peristasis of 8 × 17 Doric columns; a pronaos; a cella that was highly innovative due to the colonnade, shaped like the Greek letter *pi* in order to accommodate the colossal statue of the goddess, which would otherwise have overwhelmed a setting with traditional aisles; and an *opisthodomos* (a porch at the rear of the cella) connected to the large chamber of the Parthenon. The edifice was built with a constant ratio of 9:4 and it applied an organic system of optical correction, such as the curvature of the platforms and horizontal lines, the inclination of the columns toward the middle of the cella, and the progressive decrease of the intercolumniation and the elements of the frieze.

108 - DURING THE ARCHAIC PERIOD THE ATHENIAN ACROPOLIS, ONCE A MYCENAEAN CITADEL, BECAME THE SEAT OF THE CULT OF ATHENA, TO WHOM THE MAIN TEMPLES WERE DEDICATED.

109 - THIS GENERAL VIEW OF THE ACROPOLIS SHOWS THE AXIAL LAYOUT OF THE PROPYLAEA AND THE PARTHENON; THE ERECHTHEION IS VISIBLE ON THE LEFT.

110-111 - The perfect proportions of the Parthenon are the outcome of the collaboration of prominent figures such as Ictinus and Callicrates, supervised by Phidias; 448/47-432 BC.

111 top - This modern copy reproduces the group portraying Cecrops and his daughter Pandrosus on the west pediment of the Parthenon.

111 center - Like the Parthenon, the complex of the Propylaea designed by Mnesicles is made entirely of Pentelic marble, with insets of black stone from Eleusis; 437/46-432/31 BC.

111 bottom - Callicrates built the Temple of Athena Nike on the rampart of the Acropolis, to the right of the Propylaea, in about 420 BC.

112-113 - THE PORCH OF THE
CARYATIDS, PROBABLY THE WORK OF THE
SCULPTOR ALKAMENES, IS THE BEST-
KNOWN SECTION OF THE ERECHTHEION.

113 - THE ERECHTHEION WAS BUILT IN
THE AREA OF THE OLDEST ATTIC CULTS,
WHICH WERE GIVEN IMPORTANT SETTINGS
BETWEEN 420 AND 405 BC.

Dazzling sculptural decorations embellished the temple, which was already impressive in and of itself. Phidias created the models and personally executed some of the 94 sculpted metopes. The themes of the Battle of the Amazons on the west side, the destruction of Troy to the north, the Gigantomachy to the east and the Centauromachy to the south mythically alluded to the victory of the Greek civilization over the barbarians. The master's hand is also evident in the continuous Ionic frieze illustrating the Panathenaic procession (a revolutionary concept in a Doric building!) and in the statues of the two pediments (depicting the birth of Athena on the east side, and the contest between Athena and Poseidon for the patronage of Attica on the west side). The chryselephantine statue of Athena Parthenos was also the work of Phidias. The 40-foot-tall sculpture portrayed the goddess erect and armed. The outside of her shield bore a bas-relief of the Battle of the Amazons: the faces of its main figures, Theseus and Daedalus, were supposedly portraits of Pericles and Phidias, who were thus accused of impiety (*asebeia*), an issue that marked the beginning of Pericles' political decline. Because of its cost, roughly equivalent to that of a fleet of 200 triremes, the temple effectively represented the treasure of Athens. It was inaugurated in 438, though it was not actually completed until several years later.

The harmonious integration of the decoration of the architectural structure, the structure's function in relation to the colossal statue of Athena Parthenos, and the ties between the great statue and the sculptural cycles of the temple were the result of an extraordinary political, cultural and religious juncture that was unique in ancient history, the perfect fusion of the goddess and her city achieved with the help of the city's most dynamic figures.

The works crafted by the master represent the most intense, vigorous and magnificent touches. Above all, however, they are the most innovative in Classical art. The figures come to life through his vibrant nudes and the rich treatment of draping. His rendering of sheer and almost transparent fabrics actually seems to shape the bodies, not only with folds – dense and full in some cases, lightly rippled in others – but also with taut, flattened surfaces that almost look wet, clinging to the body as if the two had become one.

114 - THE FRIEZE AROUND THE CELLA OF THE PARTHENON PORTRAYS THE PROCESSION OF THE PANATHENIANS BEFORE THE OLYMPIAN GODS (IN THE PHOTOGRAPH, POSEIDON AND APOLLO, EAST SIDE) (ACROPOLIS MUSEUM, ATHENS).

115 TOP - ACCORDING TO TRADITION, THE AMAZONOMACHIA THAT DECORATED THE SHIELD OF ATHENA PARTHENOS INCLUDED PHIDIAS' SELF-PORTRAIT AND A PORTRAIT OF PERICLES (BRITISH MUSEUM, LONDON).

115 BOTTOM - THIS COPY OF ATHENA PARTHENOS, FOUND AT THE VARVAKEION GYMNASIUM IN ATHENS, OFFERS A VAGUE IDEA OF WHAT PHIDIAS' CHRYSELEPHANTINE MASTERPIECE MUST HAVE LOOKED LIKE (NATIONAL ARCHAEOLOGICAL MUSEUM, ATHENS).

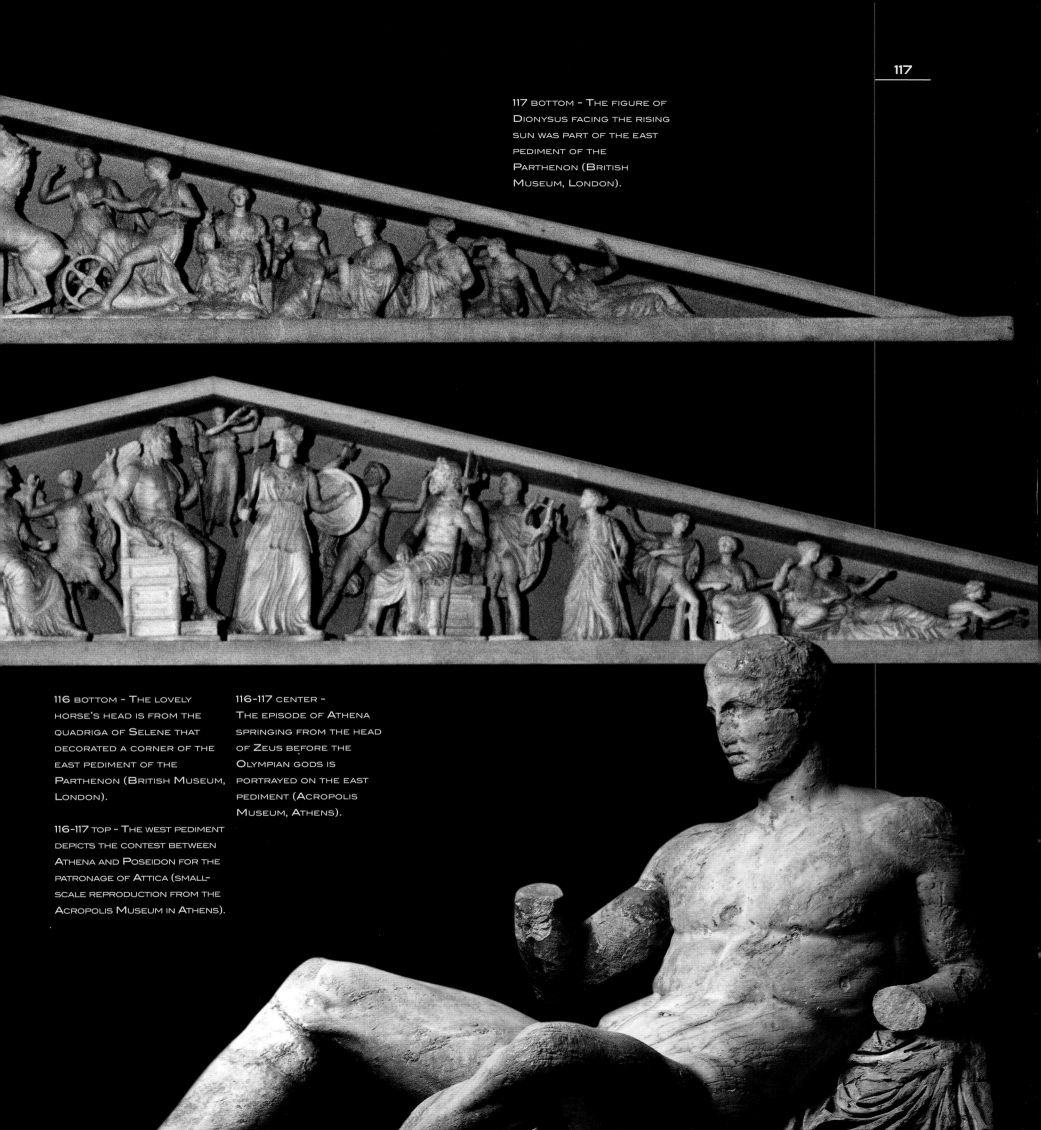

117 bottom - The figure of Dionysus facing the rising sun was part of the east pediment of the Parthenon (British Museum, London).

116 bottom - The lovely horse's head is from the quadriga of Selene that decorated a corner of the east pediment of the Parthenon (British Museum, London).

116-117 top - The west pediment depicts the contest between Athena and Poseidon for the patronage of Attica (small-scale reproduction from the Acropolis Museum in Athens).

116-117 center - The episode of Athena springing from the head of Zeus before the Olympian gods is portrayed on the east pediment (Acropolis Museum, Athens).

118-119 - The north
section of the
Parthenon frieze
represents *hydria*- and
offering-bearers
(Acropolis Museum,
Athens).

119 - In the east section,
which is slower paced,
the *ergastinai* (the
virgins responsible for
weaving Athena's peplos)
advance toward the gods
(The Louvre, Paris).

120 - This image of Artemis from the eastern frieze of the Parthenon fully depicts the humanization of the classical ideal (Acropolis Museum, Athens).

121 - The "Laborde Head" pertains to a statue of Iris from the west pediment of the Parthenon (The Louvre, Paris).

122 - The chronology of the Riace Bronzes, their artistic attribution and the identification of the figures are still being debated. Some think that they were intended for the Athenian treasury for Marathon at Delphi, some for the treasury of the Achaeans at Olympia, and others for the Monument of the Eponymous Heroes at the agora in Athens (National Archaeological Museum, Reggio Calabria).

123 - It has been suggested that Warrior B represents Miltiades or an Attic hero. The stylistic influence of Polyclitus' standards is evident. This work has been dated to about 430 BC (National Archaeological Museum, Reggio Calabria).

124 and 125 - Warrior A probably represents Agamemnon or Ajax, and has been connected with the works of the final phase of the Severe period and the beginning of Phidias' activity; ca. 460 BC (National Archaeological Museum, Reggio Calabria).

After the work at the Parthenon, Phidias was called to Olympia, where he sculpted the colossal statue of Zeus, considered one of the seven wonders of the world. He then went to Elis, where he sculpted a statue of Aphrodite and participated in the competition at Ephesus to create a figure of one of the Amazons for the local sanctuary of Artemis. He returned to Athens in about 432, where he fell victim to the opposition against Pericles. Indicted for impiety, he was thrown into prison, where he died a short time later. In addition to works such as the Apollo Parnopios, Anacreon and the Lemnian Athena, other sculptures have also been attributed to Phidias, such as the bronze statues that were part of the votive offering of the Athenians at Delphi, dedicated to the heroes of the Attic tribes. Modern scholars also think that the famous Riace Warriors were the work of Phidias. The bronze statues were lost during a shipwreck and were rediscovered several years ago in the waters off the Calabrian coastal town of Riace

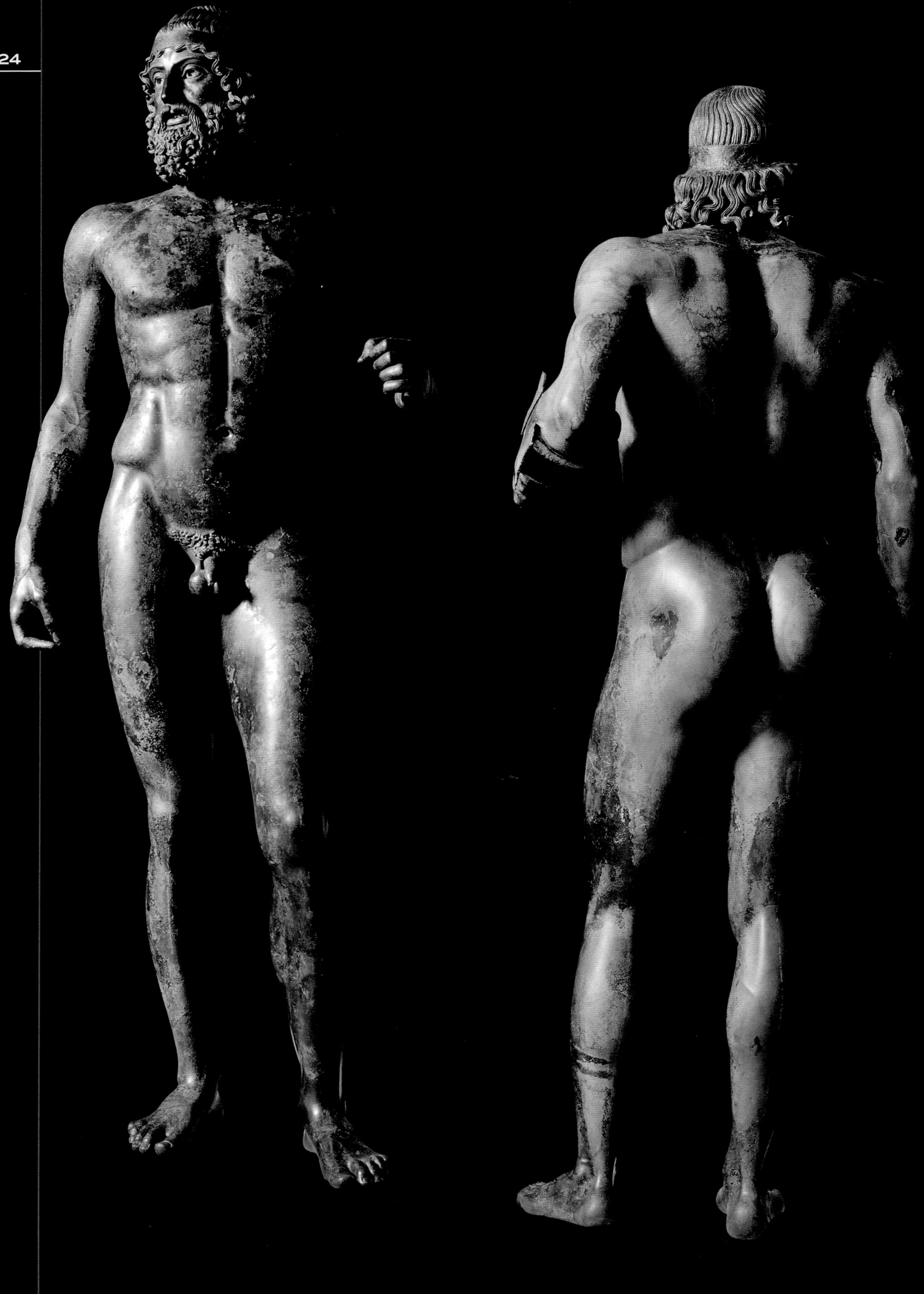

Pupils and artists involved in the great workshop of the Parthenon included the sculptors Agorakritos and Alkamenes, who launched an artistic trend that developed the Phidian style, exaggerating its most distinctive features and transforming its spirit to achieve results that can be defined as mannerist. The nudes became more anguished and drapery more pictorial, loose and fluttery, independent of the body and its movement. This approach created extraordinarily sophisticated interplays of folds and "wet" drapery, in which the lesson of the great master was merely the pretext for a virtuoso interaction between the artist and his medium, marble. Toward the end of the 5th centu-

ry, graceful dancing or flying figures were created in the Phidian style. These include the Nike of Paionio and the bas-relief figures sculpted by Callimachus on the balustrade of the Temple of Athena Nike. Timotheos' sculptures of Aura on horseback for the Temple of Asclepius at Epidaurus date to around 375.

However, the second half of the 5th century was also the period of another great sculptor, Polyclitus of Argos, whose works helped forge the male athletic ideal. We know that he studied the human figure in order to determine authoritative principles. He also wrote a treatise, *Kanon* ("Rule"), in which he dictated standards for creating a statue based on precise geometric ratios. Polyclitus' intention was to provide a system of proportions so as to create a harmonious rapport between the individual parts of the human body based on numbers, evidently influenced by the theory formulated between the late 6th and early 5th centuries by Pythagoras, who stated that numbers were the foundation of all things.

Many scholars have pointed to the *Doryphorus (Spear Bearer)* as the paradigm of these principles, though others cite the portrait of Kyniskos, the young victor of a boxing match held in Olympia in approximately 460. He also created works portraying Hermes, Heracles, a Diadumenos and an Amazon, and a colossal chryselephantine statue of Hera for the sanctuary of his city. All his works reveal a new sculptural stance, with one leg that carries the main weight and the other that is free and slightly bent. This imparts a more natural and organic definition of the rhythm with which the figure occupies space, an agile yet balanced pace constructed through a series of intersecting contrapositions of tensed and resting parts. This solution was the also the outcome of an intentional and proportionate anatomic articulation, and it is no accident that the few extant fragments of Polyclitus' treatise have been handed down through the quotations of the scientist Galen, who lived in the 2nd century AD.

Hippodamus of Miletus was yet another key figure of the "Classical," a term that evokes the idea of order, balance, harmony and measure. He was active in the area of urban planning, a field that was tied to the political sphere – in the general sense of the term – far more than it is today. Aristotle, one of the leading thinkers of antiquity, wrote in his *Politics* that Hippodamus "discovered the division of cities." What does this mean? The colonial *poleis*, founded in virgin territory during the Archaic, were immediately given a rational layout that divided space with streets intersecting at right angles.

126 - The Nike of Paionios was situated in the Temple of Zeus at Olympia; ca. 460 BC (Olympia Museum).

127 left - The *Diadumenos* is a mature work by Polyclitus; ca. 430 BC (National Archaeological Museum, Athens).

127 right - The *Doryphorus* dates back to 450 BC (National Archaeological Museum, Naples).

Within this rectangular grid, areas were divided into spaces reserved for public life, and zones for housing, production and crafts. Therefore, we cannot consider Aristotle's words an acknowledgement of the preeminence and invention of Hippodamus. They should instead be viewed as referring to an innovative approach to this divisional system that was already in place, following more logical and up-to-date criteria not only in the search for a link between democratic political ideas and the material structure of the city, divided into equal lots, but in relation to a stricter and more functional coordination of areas and public structures. It seems likely that Hippodamus proposed models that organically linked structures and areas to each other to form a sort of "urban hinge" that connected the residential quarters and provided easy access to common spaces (ports, markets, sacred areas and agoras): a concept we now refer to as "zoning." The port of Piraeus, which, according to ancient writers, was restructured by Hippodamus toward the middle of the 5th century, is an excellent example. Hippodamus perfected and codified the experience of the urban-planning school of Miletus. Tellingly, after it was destroyed by the Persians, Miletus itself was reconstructed with a similar layout, based on a lucid concept that catered to the needs of the community.

Influenced by philosophy and as a result of the development of scientific research (the treatises of the physician Hippocrates on the importance of natural and climatic conditions on human health and ways of life, including housing), residential structures were also configured based on a more orderly and articulated plan during this period. The rooms generally faced south, whereas a central courtyard and a portico to the north sheltered the main rooms of the house. Bathrooms and service areas were situated on the east and west sides. The widespread use of these principles is evident at Olynthus, on the Chalcidian Peninsula.

128 - THE *ARES* FROM THE BORGHESE COLLECTION HAS BEEN INTERPRETED AS A COPY OF ALKAMENES' STATUE FOR THE TEMPLE AT THE ATHENIAN AGORA; CA. 430 BC (THE LOUVRE, PARIS).

129 - THE *DISCOPHOROS* (DISCUS BEARER) IS A YOUTHFUL WORK BY POLYCLITUS THAT REFLECTS THE PRINCIPLES OF THE GREAT ARTIST; CA. 460 BC (STAATLICHE MUSEEN, BERLIN).

THE GREAT SANCTUARIES OF THE CLASSICAL PERIOD

Set in a "sea of olive trees," the sanctuary of Delphi was the most prestigious religious center in Greece and the "center of the universe." Used as far back as the Mycenaean period, it was transformed into a monumental site during the Archaic. However, it was during the 5th century that it became the true pantheon of Hellenic glory. The last portion of the Sacred Way, which climbed up the side of Mount Parnassus to the heart of this sacred place with the Temple of Apollo, was dotted with an impressive series of monuments celebrating joint undertakings against the barbarians. In front of the temple there was a golden tripod offered by all the Greeks to commemorate the Panhellenic victory over the Persians at Plataea in 479. This victory was also alluded to by the gift of the Tarentines for the defeat of the barbarians of Magna Graecia (the Peucetians and Iapygians). Alongside a colossal statue of Apollo, a collective gift for the victory at Salamis, there were two gold tripods offered by Gelo and

Hiero of Syracuse for their respective victories against the western barbarians, the Carthaginians at Himera in 480 and the Etruscans at Cuma in 474. Inversely, the first part of the Sacred Way offered a clear picture of the political fragmentation of the poleis, each of which tended to exalt its own prestige in a competition that was "settled" closer to the temple. Immediately after the entrance to the sacred enclosure, the votive offerings were arranged in a dense sequence, fully displaying the ideological clash between democratic Athens and Argos, and oligarchic Sparta. This dispute would leave its mark on Greek history above all in the 5th century and in part of the 4th. Consequently, the treasury built by Athens after 467 to commemorate the Battle of Marathon retrospectively celebrated the victory over the Persians in 490, but it was intended above all to emphasize the greatness and power of the Attic polis. Yet next to it was the monument of the Navarchs, built by Sparta to recall its victory over Athens in the sea battle of Aegospotami in 405. And just after this monument pilgrims would come across the Trojan

130 - THE ATHENIAN TREASURY AT DELPHI WAS PROBABLY BUILT TOWARD THE END OF THE 6TH CENTURY BC, AS DEMONSTRATED BY THE STYLE OF THE METOPE; 510-500 BC.

130-131 - THE TEMPLE OF APOLLO AT DELPHI, AS IT IS TODAY, IS THE SIXTH BUILDING AND WAS REBUILT AFTER THE EARTHQUAKE OF 373 BC.

131 BOTTOM - THE OMPHALOS WAS THE SYMBOL OF THE CENTER OF THE EARTH AND WAS SITUATED ALONG THE SACRED WAY AT DELPHI (ARCHAEOLOGICAL MUSEUM, DELPHI).

Horse, the gift of Argos for the great victory over the Lacedae-monians in 414. In response to this, a large monument was erected after 405 and it originally bore two gold stars dedicated by the Spartan general Lysander. Then there was the offering of the Arcadians, erected after the battles of Leuctra and Mantineia (first half of the 4th century), which liberated these populations from Spartan hegemony, and this was followed by the statue of Philopoemen, who victoriously led the Achaean League against Sparta at the end of the 3rd century.

This "battle of images" later became more restrained and a more subdued route was formed amidst small and precious buildings shaped like temples (*thesauroi*), in which each city safeguarded its votive offerings to Apollo. Some of them – the Sicyonian, Siphnian, Theban and Athenian Treasuries – marked the transition from the Archaic to the Classical period with their breathtaking architectures and decorations.

In the most secret part (*adyton*) of the main temple of the sanctuary, the Pythia or Sibyl, the priestess of Apollo, would sit on the sacred tripod near the opening in the earth that released vapors. These vapors, together with the laurel leaves the Sibyl would chew, would send her into a trance, in which she would lend her voice to the god and hand down obscure oracular responses. The area in which, according to myth, Apollo had founded the sanctuary was situated under the imposing terracing of the temple.

132 LEFT - THE STADIUM AT DELPHI WAS RESTORED UNDER HADRIAN. IN THE FOREGROUND: THE FOUNDATIONS OF THE ENTRANCE ARCH DEDICATED BY HERODES ATTICUS; 2ND CENTURY AD.

132 RIGHT - THE SANCTUARY OF ATHENA PRONAIA,

AT MARMARIA TERRACE (DELPHI), ENCLOSES THE *THOLOS* OF THEODOROS, DEDICATED TO THE LOCAL HERO PHYLAKOS; 380-370 BC.

132-133 - THE THEATER AT DELPHI WAS BUILT IN THE 4TH CENTURY BC.

134 AND 134-135 - THE SIPHNIAN
TREASURY, A GEM OF ARCHAIC IONIC
ARCHITECTURE, HAS YIELDED A
SPLENDID FRIEZE WITH MYTHOLOGICAL
SCENES. THE NORTH SIDE PRESENTS
THE GIGANTOMACHY, WITH A LION
BITING A GIANT (LEFT) AND ARTEMIS
DRIVING A GIANT AWAY (RIGHT).
THE EAST, WEST AND SOUTH SIDES
RECORDED THE BATTLE BETWEEN
GREEKS AND TROJANS,
THE JUDGMENT OF PARIS AND THE
RAPE OF THE DAUGHTERS OF
LEUCIPPUS; 525 BC
(ARCHAEOLOGICAL MUSEUM, DELPHI).

The "land of the Olympian" – Zeus – was also the site of another great sanctuary important to all the Greeks. Though it was connected with the famous games (776 is the date conventionally cited for the first Olympiad), more importantly it was the oracle of the king of the gods, specialized in matters of warfare.

Neither Olympia nor Delphi has yielded documentation illustrating and explaining the origins and development of these places of worship. Olympia unquestionably had monumental structures by the 5th century, notably the majestic temple built by Libon and the stadium. After the work done in the 6th century, the stadium was given an important architectural appearance that was also designed to serve as a dignified backdrop for the countless votive offerings that were brought here. Starting in the 6th century, precious *thesauroi* were gradually added be-

tween the stadium and the temple. The victories of the early 5th century over the eastern and western barbarians provided the opportunity to manifest the common pride of the Greeks – or, more often than not, of the individual poleis – with splendid votive offerings at the *thesauroi*. The 5th century was also an important period for the third great Panhellenic religious center. The cult of the healer god Asclepius has been documented at Epidaurus as early as the 6th century, but the terrible plague that broke out during the Peloponnesian War in about 430 was decisive for the spread of this cult. The sanctuary became one of the most important sacred places in the Greek world and extensive construction was undertaken, notably the Temple of Asclepius and the famous tholos. The former, built by Theodotos, held Thrasymedes' chryselephantine cult statue and was decorated with sculptures by Timotheos; the latter, built by Polyclitus the Younger, was the center for the hero cult of Asclepius. According to myth, he was the son of Apollo and the nymph Coronis, and he learned the art of medicine from the centaur Chiron. Asclepius became so skilled in healing men that he was even able

to revive the dead, and Zeus killed him with a thunderbolt because of this. Freed from his mortal body, however, Asclepius rose to Olympus and took his place among the gods. The area of the sanctuary was divided into numerous structures set up to house pilgrims and the sick. The place of treatment was referred to as the *abaton* ("unapproachable") and, following purification rituals, the ill would spend the night here, waiting for divine healing as they slept. It is widely – but wrongly – thought that the healing and oracular activities at these sanctuaries were overseen

mainly by charlatans. In reality, the cures offered took advantage of the fact the enormous numbers of "international" visitors allowed the priests/healers to amass an extraordinary amount of information on symptoms, diseases, healing methods and experimentation, and the effects of medicinal substances. Drawing on this wealth of knowledge, they could thus provide "answers" to the ill and the faithful. Though the information may have been somewhat superficial and generic, it was based on solid and widespread knowledge, and was thus quite reliable.

136 - THE ENTRANCE TO THE STADIUM OF OLYMPIA DATES BACK TO THE LATE 3RD – EARLY 2ND CENTURY BC.

136-137 - THE SANCTUARY OF OLYMPIA IS SET AROUND THE TEMPLE OF ZEUS (471-456 BC).

137 TOP - THE TEMPLE OF ZEUS, THE WORK OF THE ARCHITECT

LIBON, WAS REDISCOVERED BY A GERMAN EXPEDITION IN THE LATE 1800s.

137 BOTTOM - THE PRYTANEION WAS THE HEADQUARTERS OF THE ADMINISTRATORS OF THE SANCTUARY, AND THE WINNERS OF CONTESTS AND ILLUSTRIOUS VISITORS WERE WELCOMED HERE.

138 TOP - THE THEATER AT EPIDAURUS, ATTRIBUTED TO POLYCLITUS THE YOUNGER, STANDS ON THE SLOPES OF MOUNT KYNORTION, THE LOCATION OF THE ANCIENT CULT OF MALEAS, LATER ASSIMILATED WITH APOLLO MALEATAS; MID-4TH CENTURY BC.

138 BOTTOM - THE SO-CALLED GYMNASIUM AT EPIDAURUS IS A BUILDING DATING BACK TO THE LATE 4TH – EARLY 3RD CENTURY BC AND IT MAY HAVE BEEN USED FOR CULT BANQUETS.

138-139 - THE FAMOUS SANCTUARY OF ASCLEPIUS, THE HEALER GOD WHOSE CULT BECAME WIDESPREAD FOLLOWING THE PLAGUE THAT BROKE OUT DURING THE PELOPONNESIAN WAR, WAS LOCATED AT EPIDAURUS.

THE PELOPONNESIAN WAR (431-404)

The Peloponnesian War broke out in the spring of 431, and because of its far-reaching political, economic and territorial repercussions it represents the "mother of all wars" in Greek history. The thirty-year truce of 446 was abruptly violated when Sparta, tired of Athens' repeated hostilities toward its allies, particularly Corinth (for reasons of commercial rivalry), decided to invade Attica. According to Thucydides, however, "The real cause I consider to be the one which was formally most kept out of sight. The growth of the power of Athens, and the alarm which this inspired in Lacedaemon [Sparta], made war inevitable."

During the first phases of the conflict, the Spartan general Archidamus, with an army of about 40,000 men, avoided open clashes and direct assaults on the rival city, preferring swift but devastating incursions into Attica to weaken Athenian resistance and, above all, to deplete supplies. In 430 a terrible plague broke out in Athens, felling Pericles along with a third of the Attic population. Cleon took over leadership of the democratic faction in favor of war, whereas Nicias headed the conservatives, who wanted to reach an agreement with their potential rival. When the two most ardent supporters of the hostilities – Cleon and the Spartan Brasidas – were killed at Amphipolis in 421, difficult negotiations were undertaken, ending with the Peace of Nicias. Though this did not solve the situation, it nevertheless marked an important victory for Athens, as it meant that its claim for recognition of its spheres of influence had been accepted. This alleged peace led to a sort of truce, albeit one marked by brutal episodes of violence and repression against the allies of both sides, culminating with the Athenians' massacre of the people of the island of Melos, who had refused to join the alliance against Sparta (415).

The horrors of war were soon forgotten, and the radical faction, headed by Hyperbolus and Alcibiades, gained the upper hand in Athens. With the intention of isolating Sparta completely, Alcibiades pushed his city toward an imperialistic policy, with the goal of crossing the boundaries of the Greek continent to open up to international scenarios: Persia on the one side and the western Greek areas on the other. Athens' fate was decided by the turn of events in Sicily, where a state of permanent hostility between the Dorian Greeks and other communities reigned. When Syracuse attacked Athens' ally Lentini, and Segesta, which in turn was battling against Selinus, asked the Attic *polis* for help, Alcibiades – attracted by the island's huge economic potential – opted for armed intervention. The enormous expedition sent to attack Sicily was unsuccessful, however, and after a long series of victories and defeats, it ended in disaster. The enormous losses also weakened defenses at home, and in 413 the Spartans handily occupied the fortress of Decelea, the true "gateway" for the conquest of Attica.

The oligarchic faction exploited this critical and painful moment to overturn the democratic regime in 411, replacing it with a small group known as the Council of 400, which was vested with full powers. A new wave of military failures by the oligarchic dictatorship restored democracy in Athens, and Alcibiades rose again, thanks to several brilliant victories at the Hellespont and in Ionia. Nevertheless, the Persians' support of Sparta and the defection of many cities from the Delian-Attic League definitively weakened Athenian power and led to the city's defeat at Aegospotami in 405, at the hands of the Spartan general Lysander. The terms of surrender imposed by Sparta put an end to Athenian supremacy and triggered the crisis of the polis system, at this point characterized by growing conflict and instability.

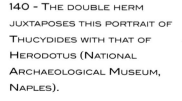

140 - THE DOUBLE HERM JUXTAPOSES THIS PORTRAIT OF THUCYDIDES WITH THAT OF HERODOTUS (NATIONAL ARCHAEOLOGICAL MUSEUM, NAPLES).

141 - THIS FUNERARY STELE FROM SALAMIS PORTRAYS THE HOPLITES CHAIREDEMOS AND LYSEAS, KILLED DURING THE PELOPONNESIAN WAR; CA. 420 (ARCHAEOLOGICAL MUSEUM OF PIRAEUS, ATHENS).

Even in these troubled years of hatred and cruelty, the Greek spirit demonstrated unfailing creativity.

In theater, for example, after the great tragedies about mythical deeds (Sophocles' *Antigone* is one of the finest examples) and the struggles against the barbarians (Aeschylus' *Persians*), works that reflected the problems and ideals of the polis continued to be staged. At the same time, Euripides' tragedies unquestionably made a deep impression on audiences through their provocations, tones and desecrating opinions about conventional ideas, proposing a rational and psychological reinterpretation of myths. Above all, however, comedy – as the free expression of the word (*parrhesia*) as an instrument to influence public opinion – probed political and cultural issues, making fun of men of power (the demagogue Cleon, for example), who were distorted to achieve comic and grotesque results. Aristophanes was the master of this genre.

The advent of sophistry was decisive in the development of the Hellenic mentality. This new and unconventional doctrine placed man at the center of things, introducing a worldview that revolved around the interest in human nature and the workings of the mind. On a very different level, through his dialectical method of inquiry Socrates taught people to reason critically, undermining the certitudes of sciolists and conformists. This break with the city's traditions led to his indictment for impiety and he was sentenced to death. Hippocrates, considered the father of modern medicine, investigated the principles and causes of disease, founding his therapeutic practices on the scientific observation of symptoms. Religion was also influenced by new ideas, as contact with the outside world gradually led the Greeks to assimilate numerous foreign cults, including the mystery cults, which during these years of profound uncertainty and suffering brought solace and even hope for eternal life.

There was also the tendency to turn to soothsayers and oracles, embrace agnosticism or even profess atheistic rationalism. In short, the convictions of traditional faith in the Olympian gods, which seemed far removed from the harsh reality of everyday life, began to crumble.

143 BOTTOM LEFT - THE SILENIC FEATURES OF SOCRATES' FACE CONVEY GREAT SPIRITUAL POWER (THE LOUVRE, PARIS).

143 BOTTOM RIGHT - THIS ROMAN HEAD, A COPY OF THE ORIGINAL FROM THE 4TH CENTURY BC, PORTRAYS HIPPOCRATES, THE MOST FAMOUS PHYSICIAN OF ANTIQUITY (THE LOUVRE, PARIS).

142 - THE DETAIL OF THE KRATER DECORATED BY THE EUMENIDES PAINTER TAKES UP A SCENE DRAWN FROM AESCHYLUS' TRAGEDY OF THE SAME NAME. IN THIS SCENE, CLYTEMNESTRA'S GHOST APPEARS TO THE TWO FURIES SLEEPING NEAR ORESTES, WHO IS PETITIONING THE SANCTUARY AT DELPHI; EARLY 4TH CENTURY BC (THE LOUVRE, PARIS).

143 TOP LEFT - THIS PORTRAIT OF SOPHOCLES EMBODIES THE MORAL IDEAL OF THE CITIZEN (NATIONAL ARCHAEOLOGICAL MUSEUM, NAPLES).

143 TOP RIGHT - THE PORTRAIT OF EURIPIDES FROM THE FARNESE COLLECTION IS A COPY THE ORIGINAL LOCATED IN THE THEATER OF DIONYSUS IN ATHENS (NATIONAL ARCHAEOLOGICAL MUSEUM, NAPLES).

THE 4TH CENTURY

THE EVENTS

The year 404 marked the end of Athenian hegemony and the Delian-Attic League was dissolved. Backed by Sparta, an oligarchy of 30 men was installed in Athens. Though they had actually been assigned to draw up a new constitution, they took extremely harsh and violent action against the members of the democracy, eliminating all its representatives – and going down in history as "the Thirty Tyrants." A group of refugees, led by Thrasybulus, finally drove out the reactionary extremists and restored democracy (403).

As Sparta extended its control across Greece, gaining few supporters in the process, in the east Persian power rose again under Artaxerxes (465-425). Taking advantage of anti-Spartan sentiment, the Persian king backed a coalition composed of Athens, Thebes, Argos and Corinth, which defeated Sparta at Cnidus in 394. Following the peace treaty the Spartan Antalcidas signed with the Persians (386), the latter regained control over the Greek cities of Asia Minor, acknowledging Sparta's dominion over the Greek mainland. The treaty also called for the breakup of all leagues with the exception of the one led by the Lacedaemonians, as they had established important alliances in central Greece. This led to extensive interference by the Spartans in the affairs of the different *poleis*, in which oligarchic regimes had essentially been installed. To counter this situation, Athens attempted to reorganize a new naval league in 377. However, Thebes, in Boeotia, also rose to a dominant position following the revival of the Boeotian League. Though Sparta may have been prepared to accept Athens' naval supremacy, it was unwilling to permit another polis to challenge its control of the mainland. The two cities ultimately went to battle in 371. At Leuctra, using an "oblique phalanx" (a new

combat strategy that bolstered the left wing of the phalanx, trained for a diagonal attack) the Theban military leaders Pelopidas and Epaminondas won a victory that dealt the final blow to Spartan military power, which was waning by this time. The Peloponnesus faced a period of instability and disorder, and in 370 the Arcadians established a federal state headed by Mantineia, whereas the Messenians founded an independent state. Sparta had seen its heyday.

Nevertheless, Theban supremacy lasted only a few years – until 362 – when the two leaders and politicians of the Boeotian city were killed in battle, Pelopidas at Cynoscephalae against the Thessalian tyrant Alexander of Pherae, and Epaminondas at Mantineia against the Spartans.

The fact that the historian Xenophon ended his *Hellenica* with the Battle of Mantinea is clearly significant, for the event represented a critical point in the history of the polis. As H. Bengston pointed out in his *History of Greece*, this political system was unable to develop the vitality that Greece desperately needed to revive a seriously deteriorated political, social and economic situation. Even the idea of a "universal peace" (*koine eirene*), which became widespread in the early 4th century and was essentially antithetical to that of the polis, did not manage to transform the political picture of the country and remained little more than the expression of a longing for peace. The basic principle of autonomy of the city-state or polis hindered the establishment of larger organizations (such as leagues) and made it impossible for them to endure. Nevertheless, the polis represented a fundamental experience, for within it man became aware of his rights and duties in society, and of his destiny as a "political animal."

144 - THE ANASTOLE, A HAIRSTYLE IN WHICH THE HAIR FANS OUT FROM THE FOREHEAD, IS A DISTINCTIVE FEATURE OF THE PORTRAITS OF ALEXANDER THE GREAT (BRITISH MUSEUM, LONDON).

146 - THE DECORATION OF THIS PART OF THE HELMET (CHEEK GUARD) PORTRAYS A SIEGE, IN A LANGUAGE RESEMBLING THE MANNERIST STYLE;

2ND HALF OF THE 4TH CENTURY (THE LOUVRE, PARIS).

147 - THE FUNERARY STELE OF DEMOCLIDES, SON OF DEMETRIUS, PRESENTS THE IMAGE OF THE YOUNG ATHENIAN HOPLITE KILLED IN A NAVAL BATTLE DURING THE WAR AGAINST SPARTA IN 394 BC (NATIONAL ARCHAEOLOGICAL MUSEUM, ATHENS).

148 - The so-called "Benevento Head" represents the classical image of a young athlete; 1st half of the 4th century BC (The Louvre, Paris).

149 - The central acroterion of the west pediment of the Temple of Asclepius at Epidaurus – representing Nike holding a bird partridge, though others think the figure represents Epione – shows the mannerist influence of the post-Phidias movements; ca. 375 BC (National Archaeological Museum, Athens).

The Peloponnesian War sparked the crisis of an ideal of civilization and a political system that had been around for centuries. The profound upheaval of social structures affected customs and outlooks. At the same time, the political decline of Athens and its loss of economic power also had serious repercussions in the field of the figurative arts. The city, which had long been a point of reference and a hub for the leading artists of the Greek world, lost its appeal after the war, and important public and private monuments were no longer commissioned here.

Yet there was also a positive element in this, represented by the break with the conventionalism, conservatism, political and social conditioning, and ensuing shift to middle-class values that had developed like a "bad seed" in the metropolis, inhibiting the influx of new ideas from the Peloponnesus, Ionia and the islands. For many years, the lack of a true dominant center was also felt in the artistic field, and the new political organizations such as the leagues showed little interest in commissioning artwork.

As a result, traveling artists and workshops became common. No longer tied to the individual *polis* that had formerly given them specific indications about the works to be executed, artists were free to cultivate personal trends, developing forms of self-awareness and vibrantly affirming their personality. Citizens and artists alike discovered themselves and their place in a multifaceted world, and the latter began to open up to their innermost sentiments and passions, experimenting extensively. At the same time, however, they did not reject the past, acknowledging its consummate value as the "Classical" model to be followed as a point of reference and guidance. The experiences of the 4th century fluctuated between these two extremes.

THE FIGURATIVE ARTS

152 - DEXILEOS, A 20-YEAR-OLD HORSEMAN WHO DIED NEAR CORINTH, IS SHOWN AS HE CHASES HIS ADVERSARY; CA. 390 BC (CERAMICS MUSEUM, ATHENS).

153 - THE PELOPONNESIAN WAR LED TO A SHARP DECLINE IN THE NUMBER OF PUBLIC MONUMENTS, AND SKILLED ARTISANS BEGAN TO WORK FOR PRIVATE CUSTOMERS. THE FUNERARY STELE OF MENSARETE IS AN EXAMPLE; 380-360 BC (STAATLICHE ANTIKENSAMMLUNGEN UND GLYPTOTHEK, MUNICH).

At first glance, the 4th century seems to be one of continuity in the arts, reinterpreting the great Classical creations to represent a second or late revival of this style. However, closer investigation of its artistic manifestations shows that it was a period of significant vitality, innovation and creativity, with movements that marked a true renaissance. Once again, Athens provides an ideal vantage point.

Even smaller monuments, such as the funerary stele of Dexileos (394), took up the figurative motifs of the Classical Parthenonic repertory, but at the same time they showed a new – though veiled – attention to pathos in the bond between the glances of the figures. The stele of Mnesarete, carved a short time later (380), also strives to forge a connection between the figures, choosing the register of shared but unspoken sadness. A large statue erected in the agora just after 375 depicts Eirene, the goddess of peace, holding the infant Plutus, representing the wealth generated by peace. This work takes up Classical concepts and elegantly softens them to express the desire for peace of this period, but at the same time it creates a close bond between the two figures, separating them from the world around them.

All these works convey a sense of isolation and detachment between the work of art and the observer's world outside. This ushered in a trend that seemed to favor the manifestation of sentiment, mood and pathos, and it reached its highest expression with Scopas. Even the traditional deities of Olympus were no longer represented in solemn apparitions, but reflected more reserved and withdrawn attitudes closer to everyday life, humanizing the Classical ideal. Artists strived for grace (charis), sensuality, soft naturalism and fluid rhythm, qualities epitomized by the works of Praxiteles. Lysippus developed the rational principles of Polyclitus regarding proportions, introducing "optical" canons that were less abstract and more human and natural, and underscoring the concept of individuality.

During the Archaic and Classical periods, solidity and solidarity were extremely strong among the social body (even in tyrannical regimes). As a result, each citizen identified himself with the political and religious institutions; rules were not viewed as restrictive but simply as guidelines that helped achieve consensus. The celebration of public figures in statues and portraits was bound by strict elements, so that there was a distinctive portrait/type for the strategist, the priest, the philosopher and so on. In this more secular and "bourgeois" world dominated by individualism, the realistic and true-to-life portrait became fashionable, affirming the importance of personality and the human mind.

154 - According to several scholars, *Hermes and the Infant Dionysus*, which Pausanias cited as the work of Praxiteles, was executed toward the end of the master's career; 335-330 BC (Archaeological Museum, Olympia).

155 - The supple grace of Praxiteles' work is evident in *Apollo Sauroktonos* ("lizard slayer"); ca. 360 BC (The Louvre, Paris).

One of the best-known figures in ancient art was the Athenian Praxiteles, the son of Cephisodotus, who sculpted the statue of Eirene and Plutus. His authorship of a large series of works has been confirmed, and many others have been attributed to his workshop because of their unique and highly personal style. Whereas the figurative model is rather conventional – the figure is almost always resting against a support – and the viewpoint is fixed and specific as a result, his works are unmistakable because of their fluid lines, elegance, spiritual expression and the sensuality of his figures.

In his *Resting Satyr* Praxiteles dissolved Polyclitan rhythm in a refined and graceful S-shaped pose – taken up again in *Apollo Sauroktonos* ("lizard slayer") – whereas his portrayal of the god as a delicate young boy, completely absorbed in his game, was completely new. In this work, the support is essential for balance. The soft, fleshy body of the resting Satyr is released entirely onto the support of a column; the animal pelt thrown over his shoulder enhances the brightness of his body by contrasting with it. Praxiteles' most famous work is his Cnidian Aphrodite, and this marks the first time the goddess was portrayed in an utterly human moment. Free of any constraints, the goddess moves in a sphere far from men, and her pensive and dreamy gaze reveals no sense of familiarity with the observer. In this case as well, her lithe and slender body – dazzling in its nudity – contrasts with the vivid effect of the secondary element, the vase on which the goddess sets her gown before bathing. In all of Praxiteles' sculptures, contrast is heightened by the different essence of the naked body: its soft and fleshy surfaces, muted by the subtle transition of planes that delicately and smoothly capture light, are offset by the rough texture and rich chiaroscuro of the support, the tresses and the accessories.

The deities were no longer viewed as mystical incarnations of abstract and mysterious forces, but as the essence of intense and almost romantic humanity: figures were captured in an abandoned and intimate dimension. The sadness that veils most of his works – including the extraordinary *Apollo Lyceius* – seems to be that of one who senses the end of a glorious era.

THE GREAT MASTERS OF SCULPTURE

HISTORY AND TREASURES OF AN ANCIENT CIVILIZATION

Scopas, the master of pathos, was just the opposite in temperament. Born on Paros, he spent time in Athens, where he learned Classical concepts and then went to the Peloponnesus, where he also worked as an architect – at the temple of Athena Alea at Tegea – and at Halicarnassus in Asia Minor. His figures, which were always sustained by an organic structure, are rendered with immense though sometimes exaggerated vibrancy, and complex rhythms expressing passion and inner tension. His *Maenad* is overcome by Dionysian *enthousiasmos*: her head is tilted back, her loose hair tumbles down her back, and her light gown is violently torn on one side to reveal her tense body. *Pothos*, the personification of desire, fully represents the artist's interest in expressive research, which explodes in all its intensity in the splendid head from the original decoration of the temple at Tegea, animated by inner vitality and strength, and concentrated in the deep-set eyes, the furrowed brow and the nervously parted mouth. A frenzied and sometimes uncontrollable rhythm, created with contrasting diagonal lines, can be seen in some of the panels with Amazonomachia scenes that decorated the famous Mausoleum of Halicarnassus, where Scopas worked with other 4th-century masters such as Timotheos, Leochares and Bryaxis.

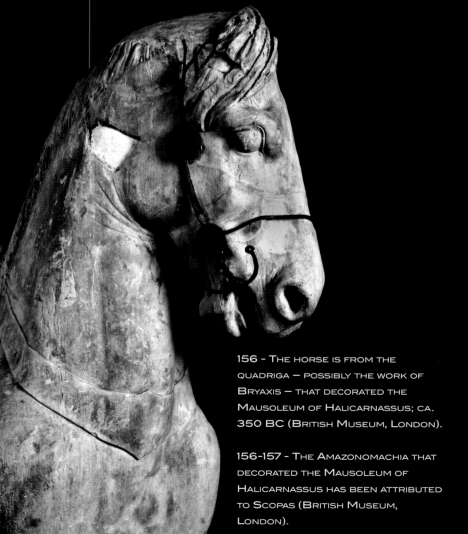

156 - THE HORSE IS FROM THE QUADRIGA – POSSIBLY THE WORK OF BRYAXIS – THAT DECORATED THE MAUSOLEUM OF HALICARNASSUS; CA. 350 BC (BRITISH MUSEUM, LONDON).

156-157 - THE AMAZONOMACHIA THAT DECORATED THE MAUSOLEUM OF HALICARNASSUS HAS BEEN ATTRIBUTED TO SCOPAS (BRITISH MUSEUM, LONDON).

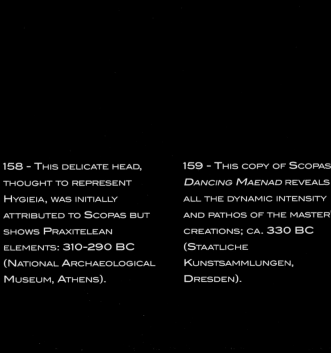

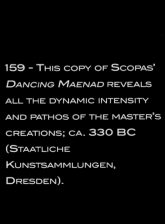

158 - THIS DELICATE HEAD, THOUGHT TO REPRESENT HYGIEIA, WAS INITIALLY ATTRIBUTED TO SCOPAS BUT SHOWS PRAXITELEAN ELEMENTS: 310-290 BC (NATIONAL ARCHAEOLOGICAL MUSEUM, ATHENS).

159 - THIS COPY OF SCOPAS' *DANCING MAENAD* REVEALS ALL THE DYNAMIC INTENSITY AND PATHOS OF THE MASTER'S CREATIONS; CA. 330 BC (STAATLICHE KUNSTSAMMLUNGEN, DRESDEN).

The crisis of the *polis*, Greece's political weakness (which was not resolved by the leagues or confederalism) and the new Persian threat paved the way for the hegemony of Macedonia. This outlying region, whose populations the Greeks considered semi-barbarian, was ruled by a feudal monarchy, with a king who came from the landed aristocracy of the "companions," the *hetairoi*. The ruling class had become profoundly Hellenized during the Late Archaic and Classical periods, and during the first half of the 5th century Alexander I, known as "the Philhellene," abolished the tribute imposed by Persia. During the Peloponnesian War, Macedonia was allied with Athens, and toward the end of the 5th century King Archelaus transformed Pella into a center of Greek culture that attracted artists and poets, including the great Euripides. This acculturation process was accompanied by the progressive expansion of military structures through which noble cavalrymen flanked heavy infantrymen with devastating power: the famous phalanx armed with the *sarissa* (a pike over 16 feet long) and organized into "units" (*syntagmata*) of 256 foot soldiers arranged in 16 rows of 16 elements.

The management of power was characterized by a fiery climate of rivalry, plots and usurpation. Philip II rose to the throne in 359. A man of great political acumen who was extremely skilled in affirming the "Greek" power of his kingdom,

he came onto the international scene as an ally and protector of Hellenism, participating in one of the many Sacred Wars for political and economic control of the sanctuary at Delphi. In 346 he finally managed to take over the Delphic Amphictyony ("League," or "those "dwelling around").

Athens was under the illusion that it could keep Macedonian aggression in check by exploiting it against Persia. In fact, the orator Isocrates wrote a pamphlet entitled *To Philip*, in which he exhorted the king to lead the allied forces of the Greeks against the Persian enemy. Demosthenes, a leading figure in Athenian law courts, made a less naive but desperate appeal. In his public speeches, the *Philippics*, the orator railed against Philip the Macedon, accusing him of posing a grave danger to Greek freedom. The "republic of orators" – as Athens was known – even formed an alliance with its old enemy, Thebes, to stand up to Philip's offensive, but the inevitable clash ended with the terrible defeat of the Greeks in the Battle of Chaeronea in 338.

Now master of the entire area, the Macedonian king established the League of Corinth, which was purely a puppet system used to control the allies, and he set about preparing an expedition against the Persians. When everything had been decided and preparations were underway, however, Philip was murdered in 336 as part of a conspiracy, and his young son Alexander rose to the throne.

THE MACEDONIAN MONARCHY AND THE END OF THE POLIS

160 - THE WORK KNOWN AS ALCIBIADES HAS BEEN ACKNOWLEDGED AS A COPY OF A GREEK WORK FROM 340 BC, WHICH MAY BE A PORTRAIT OF PHILIP II OF MACEDON. THE COPY DATES BACK TO THE 1ST CENTURY AD (CHIARAMONTI MUSEUM, VATICAN CITY).

161 - PHILIP II GAINED POSSESSION OF THE RICH GOLDMINES OF MT. PANGEUS SOON AFTER HE ROSE TO THE THRONE. THE OBVERSE OF THIS GOLD STATER DEPICTS A BIGA, ALLUDING TO THE PANHELLENIC GAMES AT DELPHI (BRITISH MUSEUM, LONDON).

The 18-year-old, who had studied literature and science under Aristotle's tutelage, showed great leadership ability as the commander of the cavalry charge at Chaeronea. Upon his father's death, he displayed steely determination in managing this difficult succession, eliminating internal adversaries and quashing the rebellious Thessalians, Thebans and Athenians. He decisively took over the role of plenipotentiary of the Panhellenic League and, as the Greek he felt himself to be, was finally in a position to organize a new war of liberation against the Persians.

Though he initially continued his father's political strategies, Alexander soon demonstrated that he had more sweeping and penetrating plans in mind. His objective, which was new in both scope and perspective, was to consolidate domestic power and then extend Macedonian domination over the entire Greek world and its areas of influence. As things turned out, he surpassed his own dreams and far exceeded every expectation.

This undertaking, which began in 334, and the conduct of the first phase of his Asian campaign indicate that Alexander was fully aware that his project would not end with the liberation of the Mediterranean coasts, although attacking the naval bases of Asia Minor was essentially to avert the threat of the Persians coming to the aid of anti-Macedonian factions in Greece. This was merely the first move of an unprecedented conquest. After crossing the Hellespont, Alexander occupied Ilium (Troy) and Lampsacus, and at the River Granicus he defeated the enemy ranks, which King Darius III did not lead personally. To accentuate the Panhellenic nature of his feat, Alexander sent 300 sets of Persian armor back to the Acropolis, dedicating them to Athena. After conquering fortified harbors, including Miletus, and freeing the *poleis* of the satrapies, he took over Lycia, Pamphylia and Pisidia, and

then wintered at the Phrygian capital of Gordium. In the spring of 333 the king resumed his march of conquest, going through Ancyra (modern-day Ankara), Paphlagonia and Cappadocia. When he reached Tarsus, where he was forced to stop due to illness, he sent Parmenio and part of his army ahead to Cilicia to halt the heralded descent of the Persian forces, led by the Great King himself. Alexander joined his general, defeating Darius in the Battle of Issus. After the fall of Tyre in 332, Alexander occupied Syria and then Egypt, a key area to gain complete control over the eastern Mediterranean. Encountering no resistance, the army reached the strategic area of the Nile Delta. Openly contrasting the attitude of the Achaemenid rulers, who looked down on other religions, Alexander went to Memphis to make a sacrifice to the god Apis, and then went to the Oasis of Ammon at Siwa, where the oracle greeted him with the title of pharaoh and "son of Ammon." He founded the great port city of Alexandria in 332-331 to promote the economic revival of Egypt and create a center that would spread the Greek culture throughout Egypt.

Military operations resumed in 331, bringing the Macedonian army to the area of the Fertile Crescent, between the Tigris and the Euphrates. In the plains of Gaugamela near Nineveh, Alexander crushed the Persians and forced Darius III to flee. Taking up the policy he had used in Egypt, Alexander presented himself as the restorer of the ancient Mesopotamian monarchy and its religion, which had been violated by the Achaemenids. In return, he was acknowledged as "king of the four parts of the world." From Babylon he marched to Susa where, in a sign of great respect for the Greeks, he had the statue group of the *Tyrannicides* – stolen by the Persians in 480 – returned to Athens. He conquered Persepolis, the capital of the Pasargadae.

162 - THIS PORTRAIT OF ALEXANDER THE GREAT, FROM THE ROMAN IMPERIAL AGE, WAS PROBABLY BASED ON A BRONZE PROTOTYPE BY EUPHRANOR (STAATLICHE ANTIKENSAMMLUNGEN UND GLYPTOTHEK, MUNICH).

163 - THIS RELIEF FROM ISERNIA DEPICTS THE BATTLE BETWEEN ALEXANDER AND DARIUS, AND REPEATS THE ICONOGRAPHY OF THE MOSAIC AT THE HOUSE OF THE FAUN IN POMPEII; 1ST CENTURY BC (ARCHAEOLOGICAL MUSEUM, ISERNIA).

Giving Darius no time to rally his forces, Alexander pursued him to Ecbatana in Media and then further east to Bactria, where Darius III was murdered by the faithless satrap Bessus.

Alexander, who was king of the Persians by this time, devoted the period of 330-327 to the definitive conquest of the northeastern satrapies, marking his eastward advance with the foundation of other cities named Alexandria, one at Kandahar, one in the foothills the Hindu Kush, and another (Alexandria Eschate, "The Farthest") in Sogdiana, at the western edge of India.

The initial purpose of the expedition – vengeance – had been transformed into imperialistic and universalistic intentions. Alexander dismissed the Greek contingents and reduced the number of Macedonian collaborators in favor of the Persian nobility, and he adopted the mentality and customs of the absolute monarchies of the East. The determined opposition of his disgruntled army, which by this time had been engaged far too long in this astonishing Asian venture, forced Alexander to return to Babylon. At Susa, in 324 he held a mass marriage of Greek-Macedonian soldiers to Persian women, in an attempt to merge the two populations. At the very moment that all the populations of the Mediterranean were sending representatives to Babylon to pay him homage, when he had great plans for the future and was at the height of his unrivaled prestige, Alexander died suddenly. The cause is unknown, but it seems likely that overdrinking and other excesses were responsible. The year was 323. A fundamental period in Western history drew to a close, yet another absolutely extraordinary period was about to begin: Hellenism, which was destined to bring the Greek culture to the new world that had been "opened up" by Alexander's conquests.

164-165 - ALEXANDER THE
GREAT, ASTRIDE HIS STEED
BUCEPHALUS, REPELS
PERSIAN SOLDIERS IN BATTLE.
THE RELIEF IS PART OF THE
DECORATION ON WHAT IS
REFERRED TO AS THE
ALEXANDER SARCOPHAGUS,
WHICH WAS CRAFTED FOR A
SATRAP (POSSIBLY
ABDALONYMUS) WHOSE
POWER WAS ACKNOWLEDGED
BY THE MACEDONIAN RULER;
CA. 310 BC
(ARCHAEOLOGICAL MUSEUM,
ISTANBUL).

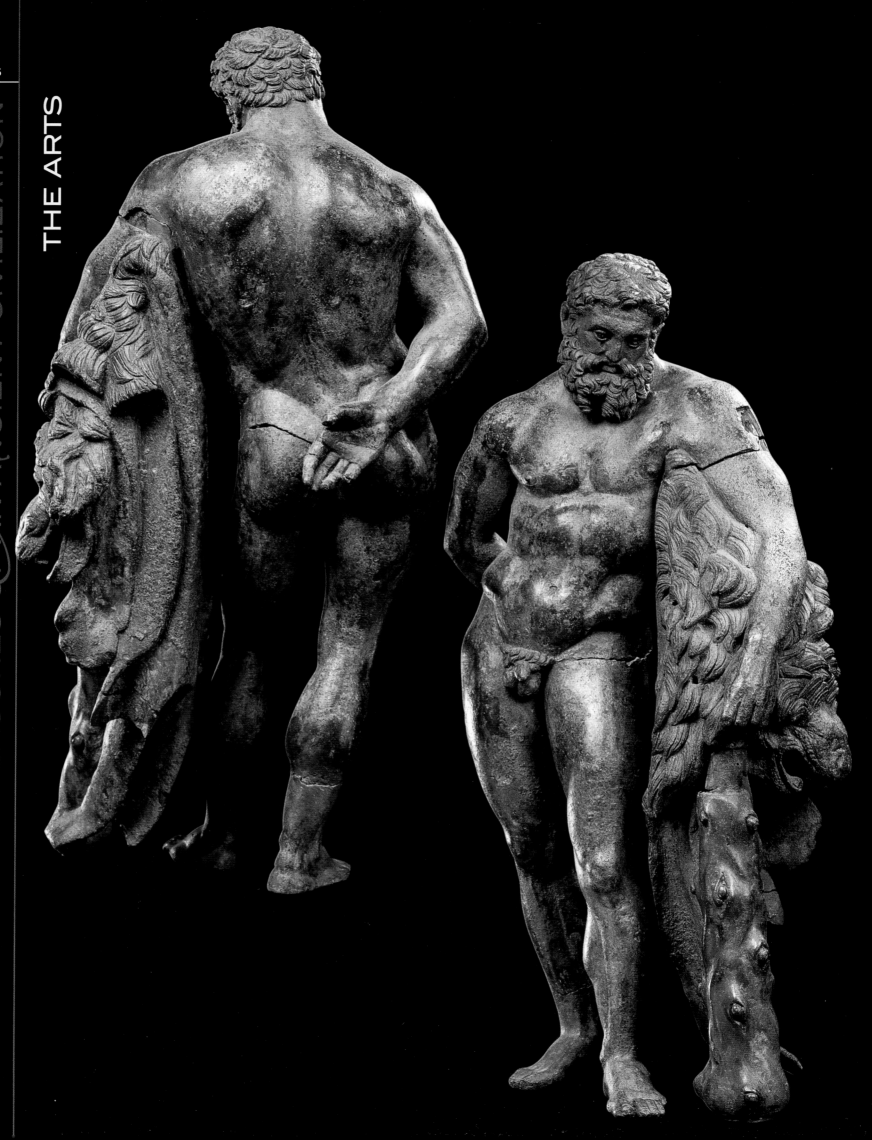

As Plato discussed the reproduction of likenesses (*phantastikè mimesis*), the sculptures of Lysippus of Sicyon cast aside the concept of art as the awareness of "being" in favor of the aesthetics of "appearing." He proposed the "optical" principle of the figure: man "as he appears to be," as opposed to man "as he is," according to the objective mode of Polyclitus (whom Lysippus indicated as his teacher, according to Pliny's *Natural History*, XXXIV, 65). A short time later, Aristotle defined the contrast between history, which reports real events, and poetry, which suggests the possible ("the poet being an imitator, like a painter or any other artist").

Therefore, Lysippus consciously drew away from anatomical standards and created smaller heads, slimmer bodies and longer legs "to give his statues the appearance of greater height," according to Pliny, who wrote that the great artist produced 150 works, mainly bronzes. This figure is probably quite accurate if we consider that many subjects were composed of large groups of men and animals, such as the one portraying the lion hunt of Alexander. Moreover, the sources indicate that Lysippus often made small-scale replicas of his statues.

We know little about his early works, but the height of his artistic activity occurred during the reign of Alexander, as Lysippus was the ruler's favorite artists and official portraitist. Toward the middle of the century, he and the painter Apelles went to Macedonia, where they also met Aristotle.

In any event, he must have enjoyed a certain amount of freedom, which allowed him to accept commissions outside the royal court. For the sanctuary of Delphi, in fact, Daochos II of Thessaly had him sculpt the statue of the athlete Agias and a group of nine statues. For the one at Thespiae, the site of Praxiteles' famous *Eros*, Lysippus sculpted *Eros Stringing his Bow*.

At the beginning of Alexander's Asian campaign, the artist was part of the leader's retinue and sculpted a group portraying the first 25 who had fallen in the Battle of Granicus. At Ephesus he sculpted Alexander with a spear, followed by his equally famous statue of Alexander on horseback. Probably to commemorate the siege of Tyre, he created *Herakles Epitrapezios* or Hercules seated. However, Lysippus soon left the great commander and did not continue the long journey to the Orient.

For Sicyon he sculpted *Kairòs*, an allegory of fortune, which may have been intended to celebrate Alexander's destiny. One of his most famous works dates back to about 323 and portrays an athlete scraping dust from his body with a strigil (*Apoxyomenos*). This work completely transforms Classical principles: the figure acquires new and supple upward movement, which culminates in the slightly raised head and thick ruffled hair. The gesture of the arms, extended forward, achieves a new sense of spatiality and a quality that is fully three-dimensional. His portrait of Socrates at the Athenian cemetery of Kerameikos is famous, and he later sculpted a portrait of Aristotle. According to a number of scholars, one of his last works was *Weary Heracles*, known through its famous copy, the Farnese Heracles, which merges pensive restlessness with the figure's titanic pose.

Another exceptional artist also captured the era of Alexander. This was Apelles, whom ancient writers considered the greatest figure in Greek painting. He executed easel paintings, as the era of large fresco murals celebrating the glories of the poleis had come to an end. The season of workshops had begun, and in these settings the painter would be surrounded by intellectuals. His most eloquent characteristic is known as the "functional line" that, together with a brilliant palette, created the illusion of volume through foreshortening. Apelles' most famous works include his *Alexander Wielding the Thunderbolt* and his *Aphrodite Anadyomene*, showing the goddess wringing out her hair as she emerges from the sea.

166 - THIS SPLENDID BRONZE REPRODUCES A FAMOUS WORK BY LYSIPPUS EXECUTED IN ABOUT 315 BC: *WEARY HERACLES* IS KNOWN THROUGH ITS COPY, THE FARNESE HERACLES. THE HERO, CAPTURED IN A MOMENT OF TIRED PENSIVENESS, HAS AN AIR OF SADNESS ABOUT HIM; ROMAN COPY (THE LOUVRE, PARIS).

167 - *EROS STRINGING HIS BOW* IS ONE OF THE FIRST MATURE WORKS BY LYSIPPUS, AND IT WAS PROBABLY MADE FOR THE SANCTUARY AT THESPIAE IN ABOUT 334 BC; ROMAN COPY (CAPITOLINE MUSEUMS, ROME).

Pella, the city chosen by Philip as his capital in place of Aigai (Vergina), offers magnificent evidence of an elevated lifestyle, with exquisite mosaics made using small river stones in natural colors. Nevertheless, modern scholars have been fascinated above all by Vergina, the remains of its palace, which are among the most notable (toward 400 King Archelaus also built a palace at Pella), and its necropolises. The tombs have yielded valuable furnishings and extraordinary paintings. The most dazzling decorations are found in the so-called Tomb of Persephone, with a scene depicting the abduction of Demetra's daughter by Pluto, the god of the underworld, and in the "royal tomb," in which Alexander and his father Philip are represented on the lion hunt. The former has been attributed to Nikomachos and the latter to Philoxenos (who also painted the original that inspired the Pompeian mosaic of the battle between Alexander and Darius, possibly at Issus). The spatial illusion that characterizes these compositions relies on a special technique that moves beyond the draftsman-like and coloristic conception of the Classical period and takes a new ap-

tall stucco frieze with battle scenes. It is topped by a pediment, showing a decisive break with the coherence and balance of the Classical period and moving toward a monumentality resembling that of the Baroque. These "ornamental façades" were destined to be popular for many years, not only in monumental architecture but also domestic structures, for the decoration of rooms painted according to illusionistic models that also laid the groundwork for the so-called "Pompeian styles." In our outline of Macedonian art, we cannot overlook the great importance of the production of luxury objects. These tombs are famous for the abundance of rich jewelry, weapons, and gold, silver and bronze vessels. Produced as part of a consolidated Hellenic tradition but distinguished by a highly elaborate Oriental and barbarian style, these objects were also splendid instruments of propaganda and exchange with the populations of the Balkan regions as far as the lands of southern Russia, inhabited by the Scythians.

168-169 - ALEXANDER THE GREAT, WITH CRATERUS (OR HEPHAESTION), IS DEPICTED ON A LION HUNT IN THE MOSAIC CREATED WITH SMALL NATURAL STONES FROM A WEALTHY ABODE IN PELLA; CA. 310 BC (ARCHAEOLOGICAL MUSEUM, PELLA).

169 TOP - PELLA BECAME THE CAPITAL OF MACEDONIA UNDER PHILIP II. IN ADDITION TO THE ROYAL PALACE AND THE AGORA, ARCHAEOLOGICAL STUDIES HAVE ALSO UNCOVERED ELEGANT HOMES.

169 BOTTOM - THE HOUSES OF PELLA ARE CHARACTERIZED BY BROAD IONIC PERISTYLES AND LOVELY MOSAIC FLOORS MADE OF RIVER STONES.

proach to chromatic values, which ancient Latin sources referred to as *pictura compendiaria*. This term seems to indicate a technique that uses rapid and simple brushstrokes rather than contour lines, creating a luminous effect through the juxtaposition of colors, which are light for the parts in the foreground and darker toward the background. In Lefkadia and throughout the entire region, the tombs show a particular architectural layout. The monumental façade, independent of the quadrangular mortuary chamber, has two levels of decorative orders (Doric and Ionic) separated by a

170-171 - THIS GOLD QUIVER FROM THE
ROYAL TOMB HAS BEEN LINKED WITH THE
VICTORY OF PHILIP II OVER THE DANUBIAN
POPULATIONS IN ABOUT 339 BC,
BECAUSE OF ITS SIMILARITIES WITH GOLD
WORK FROM SOUTHERN RUSSIA
(ARCHAEOLOGICAL MUSEUM, SALONIKA).

170 BOTTOM - THE HEAVY IRON CUIRASS
OF PHILIP WAS DECORATED WITH GOLD
FOIL (KYMATIA) AND PROTOMES OF LIONS
WITH RINGS (ARCHAEOLOGICAL MUSEUM,
SALONIKA).

171 TOP – IN THE SUPPOSED TOMB OF
PHILIP II AT VERGINA, A MARBLE CASKET
HELD A GOLD BOX WITH A LID DECORATED
WITH A *REPOUSSÉ* MACEDONIAN STAR.
THE BOX HELD THE KING'S REMAINS; CA.
340 BC (ARCHAEOLOGICAL MUSEUM,
SALONIKA).

171 BOTTOM – PRICELESS WREATHS OF
GOLD FILIGREE LEAVES AND FLOWERS
WERE SET ON THE CHESTS HOLDING THE
REMAINS OF THE DEAD (ARCHAEOLOGICAL
MUSEUM, SALONIKA).

172 LEFT - SILVER WAS THE PREFERRED MEDIUM OF HELLENISTIC TOREUTICS (THE ART OF METAL RELIEF WORK), AND VEGETAL DECORATIONS WERE GENERALLY USED; 1ST HALF OF THE 3RD CENTURY BC (BRITISH MUSEUM, LONDON).

172 RIGHT - THE TOREUTIC WORKSHOPS OF TARENTUM ACHIEVED EXTRAORDINARY LEVELS OF QUALITY IN THE 3RD CENTURY, AS DEMONSTRATED BY THE FIGURE OF APHRODITE ON THIS SILVER MEDALLION (BRITISH MUSEUM, LONDON).

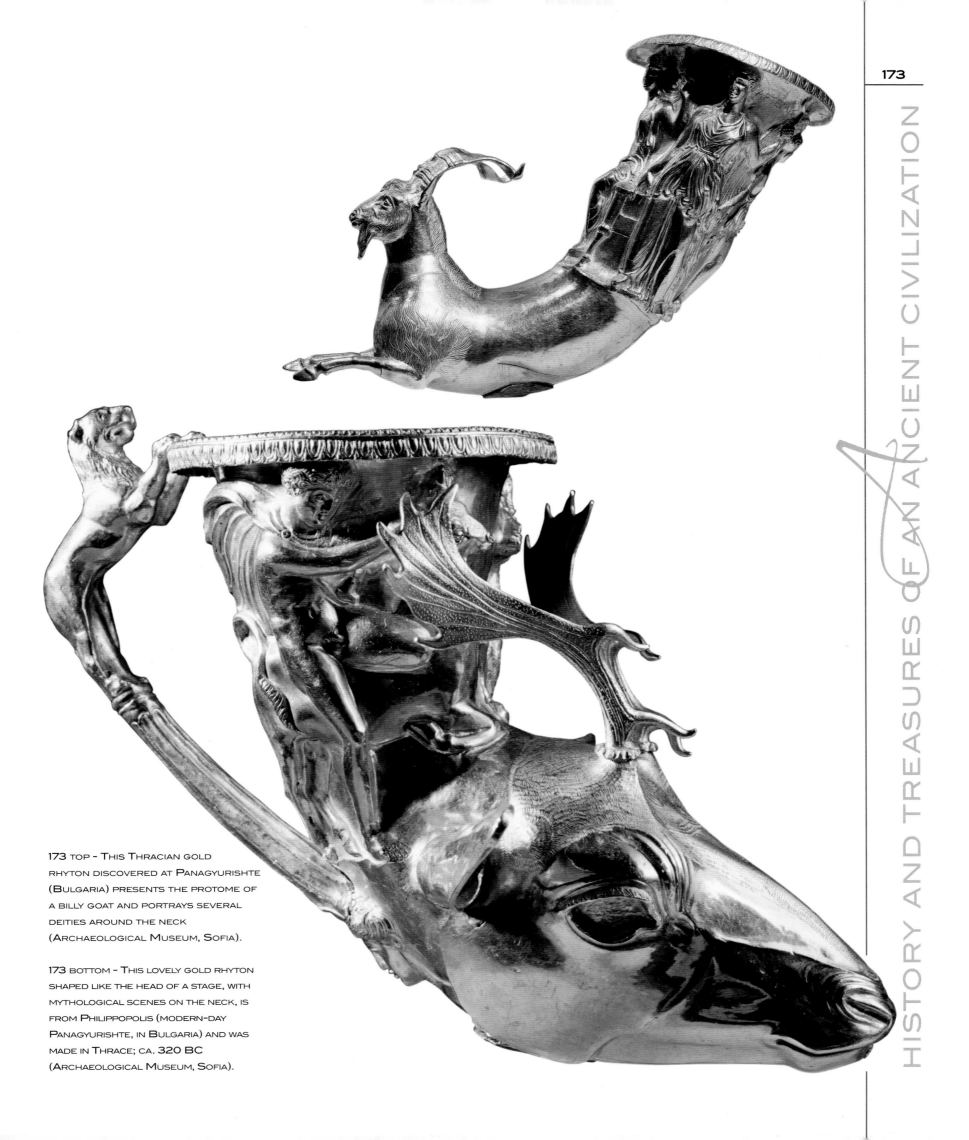

173 TOP - THIS THRACIAN GOLD RHYTON DISCOVERED AT PANAGYURISHTE (BULGARIA) PRESENTS THE PROTOME OF A BILLY GOAT AND PORTRAYS SEVERAL DEITIES AROUND THE NECK (ARCHAEOLOGICAL MUSEUM, SOFIA).

173 BOTTOM - THIS LOVELY GOLD RHYTON SHAPED LIKE THE HEAD OF A STAGE, WITH MYTHOLOGICAL SCENES ON THE NECK, IS FROM PHILIPPOPOLIS (MODERN-DAY PANAGYURISHTE, IN BULGARIA) AND WAS MADE IN THRACE; CA. 320 BC (ARCHAEOLOGICAL MUSEUM, SOFIA).

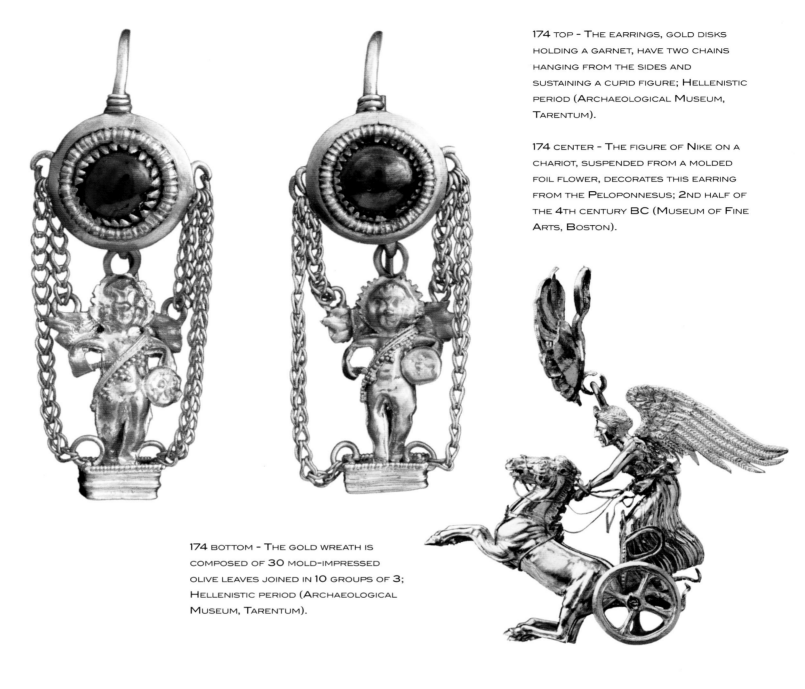

174 TOP - THE EARRINGS, GOLD DISKS HOLDING A GARNET, HAVE TWO CHAINS HANGING FROM THE SIDES AND SUSTAINING A CUPID FIGURE; HELLENISTIC PERIOD (ARCHAEOLOGICAL MUSEUM, TARENTUM).

174 CENTER - THE FIGURE OF NIKE ON A CHARIOT, SUSPENDED FROM A MOLDED FOIL FLOWER, DECORATES THIS EARRING FROM THE PELOPONNESUS; 2ND HALF OF THE 4TH CENTURY BC (MUSEUM OF FINE ARTS, BOSTON).

174 BOTTOM - THE GOLD WREATH IS COMPOSED OF 30 MOLD-IMPRESSED OLIVE LEAVES JOINED IN 10 GROUPS OF 3; HELLENISTIC PERIOD (ARCHAEOLOGICAL MUSEUM, TARENTUM).

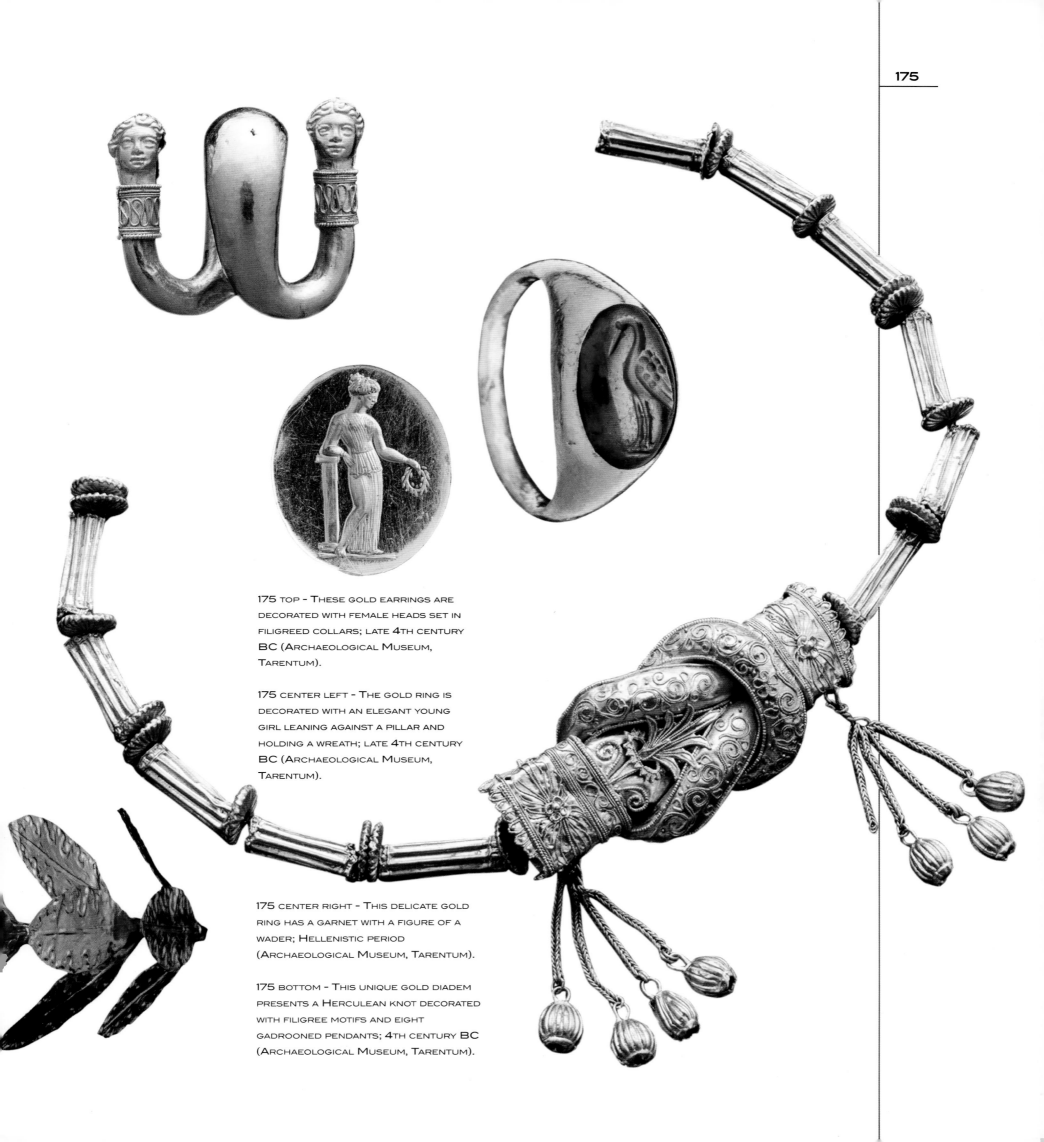

175 TOP - THESE GOLD EARRINGS ARE
DECORATED WITH FEMALE HEADS SET IN
FILIGREED COLLARS; LATE 4TH CENTURY
BC (ARCHAEOLOGICAL MUSEUM,
TARENTUM).

175 CENTER LEFT - THE GOLD RING IS
DECORATED WITH AN ELEGANT YOUNG
GIRL LEANING AGAINST A PILLAR AND
HOLDING A WREATH; LATE 4TH CENTURY
BC (ARCHAEOLOGICAL MUSEUM,
TARENTUM).

175 CENTER RIGHT - THIS DELICATE GOLD
RING HAS A GARNET WITH A FIGURE OF A
WADER; HELLENISTIC PERIOD
(ARCHAEOLOGICAL MUSEUM, TARENTUM).

175 BOTTOM - THIS UNIQUE GOLD DIADEM
PRESENTS A HERCULEAN KNOT DECORATED
WITH FILIGREE MOTIFS AND EIGHT
GADROONED PENDANTS; 4TH CENTURY BC
(ARCHAEOLOGICAL MUSEUM, TARENTUM).

5

HELLENISM

By convention, historians date the beginning of Hellenism to the year 323 BC and the death of Alexander the Great, and its end to the year 31 BC, with the Battle of Actium and the rise to power of Augustus, the future Roman emperor. However, it is more difficult to establish strict chronological boundaries for the artistic development that characterized the era. When Alexander came onto the scene, new developments were already well underway – as we have seen – and it is not easy pinpoint when they came to an end. Indeed, the great and generally uniform Hellenistic art movement effectively encompassed a number of different trends.

It has been said that Alexander's "Greek adventure" and the conquest of the *Oikoumene*, or the known world, is essentially a paradox, because the new world that was thus created did not achieve true political and structural unity until the very end, when the Pax Romana brought it into the sphere of influence of the new Mediterranean power. Nonetheless, political and administrative diversities were accompanied by extraordinary unity in terms of culture.

The terms "Hellenism" and "Hellenistic" originated on a linguistic level. The verb *hellenizein*, first used by Thucydides, refers to the adoption of Greek by barbarian populations; *hellenismóós* means "to speak Greek" rather than barbarian tongues. By extension, these terms came to indicate a culture that was more highly developed than others. Therefore, we could use the word "Hellenism" to define an era and its culture, literary and otherwise: a sphere in which a common language, an evolved and late form of Greek, was used. With specific reference to art, it can be used to refer to Greek production in its later and more advanced forms, with respect to the artistic cultures of the different geographical areas that came into contact with the Greek-Macedonian culture. Alexander's death posed the problem of his succession, which should formally have gone to his half-brother Philip Arrhidaeus or to the unborn son of the great Macedonian

ruler and the Oriental princess Roxana. In reality, Alexander's own generals proclaimed themselves his "heirs" or "successors" (*diadochoi*) and split up his empire for themselves. Antipater became the ruler of Europe (Philip and the young Alexander IV were murdered), Ptolemy took Egypt, Antigonus took Anatolia, Lysimachus took Thrace, and Seleucus became the ruler of Syria a short time later. The political line of Antigonus, who intended to reestablish a single kingdom, was violently opposed by the others. Therefore, once Antipater's victory over Athens in the Lamian War had finally quenched the libertarian spirit of all of Greece, the struggle between Antigonus, backed by his son Demetrius Poliorcetes, and the other *diadochoi* began. The victory of the Antigonus and his son over Ptolemy at Salamis, in Cyprus, did little to solve the situation. In fact, their self-proclaimed kingships immediately prompted the others to follow suit. After Antigonus was killed in Phrygia, his son Demetrius took the crown of Macedon, only to be captured by Seleucus and killed. The same fate was in store for Lysimachus. In 280, following the death of Ptolemy of Egypt (284), the murder of Seleucus eliminated the last of Alexander's officials. At this point, there were three great monarchies on the international chessboard: the Antigonid in Macedonia, the Seleucid in Asia and the Ptolemaic in Egypt. Subsequently, the Attalids of Pergamum gained their independence from the Asian kingdom. Inspired by the idea of great power modeled after the Oriental system, they were true hereditary monarchies, dynasties that were generally respectful of the national traditions of their Egyptian or Asian subjects. With the second generation of rulers, in about 280 there was a balance of power. In the meantime, however, the threat of the Celts arrived from the northwest, bringing death and destruction into the heart of Greece and then to Asia Minor, and these tribes fully demonstrated their powerful warfare tactics (Brennus' descent through Italy in 390, more than a century earlier, and the sack of Rome represent a good example).

176 - THIS PIECE IS PART OF THE GROUP OF THE THREE GRACES FOUND AT THE BATHS AT CYRENE (MUSEUM OF CYRENE).

178 - ON THE COINS OF DEMETRIUS POLIORCETES, THE RULER'S PORTRAIT IS JUXTAPOSED WITH THE FIGURE OF POSEIDON OR NIKE ON A SHIP, AS SEEN ON THESE TETRADRACHMS FROM SALAMIS IN CYPRUS (BRITISH MUSEUM, LONDON).

179 - COMPARISONS OF COINAGES HAVE MADE IT POSSIBLE TO IDENTIFY THIS BRONZE PORTRAIT FROM HERCULANEUM AS SELEUCUS I NICATOR, KING OF SYRIA; ROMAN COPY AFTER A WORK BY LYSIPPUS (ARCHAEOLOGICAL MUSEUM, NAPLES).

The term Epigoni refers to Alexander's later successors, who were also involved in long and debilitating struggles for the supremacy of their respective kingdoms (there were six Syrian Wars). At the end of the 3rd century, Antiochus III of Syria emerged as the leading figure. He was known as Antiochus the Great because of his expedition against the Persian satrapies, going as far as India and effectively taking up the legacy of Alexander the Great. Macedon's domination of Greece was transformed into full-fledged occupation in 262: during the Chremonidean War – named after Chremonides, who proposed the final peace treaty – the coalition led by Athens was forced to surrender. Subsequent attempts to regain independence, including the one by the Spartan Cleomens III in 227, were always thwarted by the Macedonians' enormous power. Toward 220, with their "allies" (including the Achaean League) the Macedonians clashed with the Aetolian League, which was backed by Sparta. The outcome was a terrible period of devastation and sacking that further debilitated the already weakened peninsula. The Peace of Naupactus in 217 is recalled as the last treaty stipulated solely among Greeks, as Roman power was looming on the horizon. The Romans had already intervened

several years before in Illyria to protect its trade interests in the Adriatic, establishing a protectorate over several cities and islands in the area with a peace treaty stipulated in 228. This worrying situation drove King Philip V of Macedon to ally himself with the Carthaginian Hannibal in 215. This led to the First Macedonian War (215-205), which ended with the Treaty of Phoenice, and Rome's alliance with the Aetolian League, Sparta, Messenia and the Attalids of Pergamum. In 200, going against the agreement between Philip V and Antiochus III of Syria, Rome made a decision that proved to be a watershed in the politics of the entire Mediterranean. It sent a delegation to Greece and, promoting anti-Macedonian propaganda, fomented a reaction against Philip. Another war broke out, and in 197 the Roman consul Titus Quinctius Flamininus won a memorable victory over the Macedonian phalanx at Cynoscephalae. At the Isthmian Games of 196 Flamininus proclaimed the liberation of Greece. In reality, however, Rome left behind occupation forces that not only exacted heavy taxes but also systematically pillaged artwork to send back to the capital. When the troops left in 194, honors were nevertheless heaped upon Flamininus, who was even venerated at Gythion as "savior."

180 - THE SEMI-PRECIOUS STONE "CUP OF THE PTOLEMIES", MADE IN ALEXANDRIA, DEPICTS THE OBJECTS FOR A DIONYSIAN PROCESSION; 1ST CENTURY BC (BIBLIOTHÈQUE NATIONALE, PARIS).

181 - THIS CAMEO, DISCOVERED IN ALEXANDRIA, REPRESENTS TWO EGYPTIAN DYNASTIES, PERHAPS THOSE OF PTOLEMY II PHILADELPHUS AND ARSINOE II; 3RD CENTURY BC (KUNSTHISTORISCHES MUSEUM, VIENNA).

CULTURE AND SOCIETY

182 top - This terracotta mask is a copy of the original model used for theatrical performances (The Louvre, Paris).

182 bottom - This theatrical mask from the Hellenistic period represents the face of a young man wearing a wreath (The Louvre, Paris).

183 - This terracotta figurine found at Tanagra represents a boy holding a theatrical mask typical of the New Comedy (The Louvre, Paris).

Though they had no political autonomy, the cities continued to be places of culture. Thanks to their favorable position in the extensive trade network of a "globalized" economy, some of them managed to gain not only undisputed economic power, but also a privileged cultural and political position. One example is Rhodes, in the middle of the eastern Mediterranean, which thrived until at least 167, when the Romans stifled the island's prosperity and independence to develop the free port of Delos.

In a subtle balancing act between princely dynasties, Athens also maintained the high cultural and artistic level it had acquired internationally during the Classical period.

Many new cities were also founded, above all in the vast eastern areas. The great urbanistic impetus, the intensive exploitation of the territories that had been conquered and ensuing demographic development provoked profound changes in the economic systems. Wealth also spread outside the courts among the important supporters of the sovereigns and upper classes. State and private banking activities mushroomed. Wealth generated luxury and a "thirst" for art, which thus became commercial and widespread through the mass production and sale of products. The use of copies and imitations of Classical masterpieces became popular for decorating private homes.

The cultural level increased but, more importantly, culture spread to various social classes. At the same time, however, we must also note the development of a vast urban working class that was very poor and culturally marginalized. Though the courts continued to be the privileged spheres of culture, numerous centers of intellectual activity and teaching developed in the gymnasia, handing down the legacy of Athens during the Classical period. The theater as a place for imparting knowledge and the center of cultural associations also became extremely widespread. The tragedy disappeared to make way for a new genre that was better suited to the daily life of the era: the New Comedy of the Athenian playwright Menander. Libraries were established, and in addition to "university-style" teaching and the reproduction of texts, they developed scientific research (for example, Aristarchus in astronomy, Eratosthenes in geography, and Archimedes in mathematics and mechanics) and philosophical speculation (Epicureanism and Stoicism). Scientific explanations of the outside world merged with moral reflections about a troubled and constantly changing society in search of inner peace, and succor from turmoil and anxiety.

It is easy to see that in this type of environment artistic creations catered to individual rather than community needs, and that they were linked with fashion, luxury and *joie de vivre* rather than common, civic or religious ideals. As it moved away from the values of the *polis*, art also shifted from community-minded to individual, and from civic to virtuoso. At the same time, it also became highly internationalized, acquiring a "shared" quality. This created a common cultural environment (in technical terms, a *koine*) that, without overriding the richness of local schools and trends, embraced all the known lands, from the Iberian peninsula to India. In the vast artistic panorama of Hellenism, we can distinguish the stylistic traditions of the great masters of the 4th century through the works of their pupils and subsequently, those of the schools that arose. The varioustrends then mingled and the schools that developed broughtgreat eclecticism to the entire artistic production of the ancient world.

The art of Lysippus was perpetuated by his followers through magnificent forms. All that remains of the Colossus of Rhodes, by Chares, is its description in ancient sources, but Eutychides' *Tyche of Antioch* fully illustrates his reliance on the pace of the ancient master. At the same time, this work also shows the taste for allegory that, after the *Kairos*, became highly successful. The young woman with a crown of towers, personifying the city founded in 300 BC, sits pensively on a boulder at the foot of which a boy is swimming (the Maeander River). The importance acquired by portraiture is reflected in works such as the statue of the playwright Menander at the Theater of Dionysus in Athens, and the one of the orator Demosthenes, erected in the Athenian agora in about 280. This work is striking in its concentration and serried rhythm, with the folds of drapery converging toward the center of the figure, a feature that would distinguish the sculpture of the early Hellenistic period. Works such as this one, and the statue of Themis personifying order and justice, created by Chairestratos for the sanctuary at Rhamnous, demand great intellectual effort on the observer's part.

184 - THIS WORK FROM THE ROMAN PERIOD IS A SMALL-SCALE COPY OF THE COLOSSUS OF RHODES, SCULPTED BY CHARES IN APPROXIMATELY 290 BC (ARCHAEOLOGICAL MUSEUM, CIVITAVECCHIA).

185 LEFT - THE ROMAN BRONZE WAS INSPIRED BY EUTYCHIDES' STATUE OF TYCHE OF ANTIOCH,

WITH THE RIVER ORONTES, FROM THE EARLY 3RD CENTURY (THE LOUVRE, PARIS).

185 RIGHT - THE PERSONIFICATION OF THEMIS AT THE SANCTUARY AT RHAMNOUS IS THE WORK OF CHAIRESTRATOS; EARLY 3RD CENTURY BC (NATIONAL ARCHAEOLOGICAL MUSEUM, ATHENS).

In the famous sarcophagus of Abdalonymus (known as the Alexander Sarcophagus) from the necropolis of Sidon, the architectural element prevails over the figurative one. Hunting scenes alternate with battle scenes, seemingly inspired by the life of Alexander and the wars of the *diadochoi*. The quest for realism led to the use of a well-constructed concept of perspective and the addition of color, of which virtually nothing remains today. Alongside the influence of Lysippus in the construction of figures, in terms of rhythm and composition we can also find references to the frieze from the Mausoleum of Halicarnassus and thus to Scopas, but also to Praxiteles. This kind of eclecticism is also evident in many funerary stelae, above all in the Attic area.

186 and 187 - The subjects represented on the monumental Alexander Sarcophagus from the royal necropolis of Sidon reinterpret the narrative layouts of Lysippus. In this case, we find sculptural groups such as those of the Battle of Granicus and the lion hunt; ca. 310 BC (Archaeological Museum, Istanbul).

The presence of the Praxitelean school is not isolated and nor is it less significant than the Lysippan school, above all in the eastern Mediterranean area and particularly in Alexandria. The supple nude that emerges from the rippling cloth draped around the hips of the famous Aphrodite of Milos shows sinuous and dynamic ascending movement that clearly harks back to the Cnidian Aphrodite, as do the Aphrodite Landolina and the crouching Venus of Doidalsas. In Alexandria the consequences of this tradition are evident in the subtle nuances and in the attention to chromatic and surface effects in the portraits of the Ptolemaic court. Balanced and symmetrical structures evolved into centrifugal and dynamic rhythms. This was the end of an era, and for the nostalgic spirits of classicism it was "the end of art." Pliny wrote in his *Natural History* that by the 121st Olympiad (296-293) "art ceased" and it would not rise again until the 156th Olympiad (156-153).

188 and 189 - The Aphrodite of Milos or Venus de Milo, with its sinuous ascending movement, harks back to Praxiteles' Cnidian Aphrodite. The contrast between soft, delicate nudity and drapery is reinterpreted through a different juxtaposition of elements. Attributed to Rhodian art, the statue inspired an extensive series of figures of the goddess that accentuate this contrast; ca. 120 BC (The Louvre, Paris).

Classical styles. This tradition emerged in particular during the 2nd century, and scholars viewed it as the revival of the great Classical ideals. Hence the opinions of Apollodorus, who wrote a work on the history of art that was one of the main sources for Pliny and his *revixit ars* ("art lived again").

A statue of Apollo with a lyre, probably the work of Timarchides and known through numerous copies, demonstrates that the contents of this classical revival were utterly cold and lifeless, subdued with completely superficial tones and the virtuoso contrasts between soft, fleshy nudes and deeply textured tresses and drapery.

Many of the so-called "Neo-Attic" artists were actually copyists, in some cases adapting the creations of the past. Extremely skilled on a technical level, they were profoundly familiar with the styles of the great masters, whom they admired and turned to for decorative inspiration. The art of the sculptor became a trade in which one selected from a vast figurative repertory, in some cases blending it eclectically – also in terms of style – to satisfy the requests of an increasingly international and demanding clientele that continued to consider Athens the beacon of the artistic culture. In this sense, the lack or, in any event, the paucity of Archaic and Severe models in the repertory of these sculptors is indicative. They were considered too abstract, difficult and aloof in terms of content, and thus unsuitable for mass production for a large market. However, these forms – in their purity, elegance and simplicity – could be adapted in new ornamental and exterior creations that highlighted the linearity of the drapery and the hairstyles, forming a highly appreciated array of "archaizing" products. Many of the Neo-Attic workshops of the 2nd and 1st centuries BC moved to Rome, the new center of power, and in signing their works the artists proudly displayed their homeland (even if only on an artistic level) as a "guarantee of quality," such as the *Kleomenoi Athenaioi*.

190 - THE ONLY ANCIENT PART OF THIS STATUE OF APOLLO CITHAROEDUS IS THE TORSO (ROMAN COPY OF A HELLENISTIC WORK): THE REST WAS ADDED DURING THE 17TH CENTURY (NATIONAL MUSEUM OF ROME, PALAZZO ALTEMPS, ROME).

191 - THE MONUMENTAL BORGHESE VASE, A MARBLE KRATER DECORATED WITH RELIEFS DEPICTING DIONYSIAN SCENES, IS A NEO-ATTIC WORK DATING BACK TO THE LATE HELLENISTIC PERIOD. IT IMITATES THE BRONZE PROTOTYPES OF THE 4TH CENTURY (THE LOUVRE, PARIS).

A number of artists also left Athens in the 3rd century BC to move to Pergamum in Asia Minor, where at the turn of the century they inspired a highly innovative artistic movement that has been dubbed the "Pergamene Baroque." With the great treasuries that Attalus I and Eumenes II dedicated not only in the capital of their own kingdom but also at the Acropolis in Athens, and in the friezes of the famous altar completed between 180 and 160 BC, the Classical experience developed into a taste for powerful structure and vigorous sculptural qualities that

192 TOP - THE CONSTRUCTION OF THE GREAT ALTAR OF PERGAMUM WAS COMMISSIONED BY EUMENES II IN HONOR OF ZEUS SOTER AND ATHENA NIKEPHOROS. A MONUMENTAL STAIRCASE LED TO THE ALTAR, AND THE ENCLOSURE WAS DECORATED WITH AN ENORMOUS FIGURED FRIEZE (PERGAMUM MUSEUM, BERLIN).

192 BOTTOM - ATTALUS I SOTER USHERED IN A NEW, MORE INDIVIDUAL AND NATURAL WAY OF REPRESENTING THE DYNASTY; CA. 230 BC (PERGAMUM MUSEUM, BERLIN).

193 - THE MONUMENTAL FRIEZE OF THE PERGAMUM ALTAR SHOWS THE BATTLE BETWEEN GIANTS AND THE GODS; 180-165 BC (PERGAMUM MUSEUM, BERLIN).

were almost exaggerated in the heavy rendering of musculature and bold, quivering rhythm. The result was violently energetic, a cosmic force, achieved also by thrusting the drill deeply into the medium to create vivid textural effects. The monumental altar erected in honor of Zeus as a political choice (propaganda for Pergamene power) is decorated with a frieze illustrating the dramatic struggle between the gods and giants (good and evil, rationality and irrationality, Hellenism and Celtic barbarism). Inside the portico, another frieze, using a less emphatic stylistic language, portrayed the deeds of Telephos, the mythical founder of the Pergamene dynasty.

Naturally, such powerfully original and expressive language was extremely successful. In Rhodes, in particular, there developed a school that made contrasting, exaggerated and centrifugal rhythms its stylistic hallmark. Works such as the famous *Laocoön Group* and the groups from Sperlonga depicting the myth of Odysseus and the punishment of Dirce are attributable to this school.

Far removed from all this – but equally significant in its expressive innovation – was the trend that modern scholars have termed the ancient "Rococo." The famous *Boy Strangling a Goose*, the work of Boethos (ca. 180 BC), can be considered the epitome of this style. In the playful tone of an epigram, a chubby boy engages in a merry but challenging battle with a downy goose, forming a pyramidal structure. Another group portrays the goddess Aphrodite intently rejecting the eager advances of a hirsute Pan, as she coquettishly brandishes her sandal to strike her assailant. Likewise, the pictorial group of the marine Centaur with Nereids and cherubs imaginatively and almost whimsically blends human and animal forms.

The insular environment of Rhodes, Delos and Cos encouraged the formation of important centers of sculpture. These islands can also be credited with inspiring the transparent rendering of clothing that was so widely praised by the ancient sources (the *Coae vestes* were famous) and that is beautifully exemplified by the statue of Cleopatra from Delos (140-135 BC), in which the different weights of the mantle and the chiton beneath create a refined interplay of transparency in swathing the opulent and sensuous body. The masterpiece of Rhodes is the celebrated *Nike of Samothrace*, now in the Louvre, with the powerful dynamism that animates this figure, with her light garment fluttering in the wind as she stands on the prow of a ship (ca. 190 BC). The same virtuoso grace and elegance animates the exquisite series of terracotta works known as Tanagra figurines, named after the city in Boeotia that was the most active production center for these items. The Rhodian Philiskos created a group representing the nine Muses. A reflection of this work, which ended up in Rome, can be glimpsed in the Archelaos Relief, dated approximately 130 BC.

194 - THE FAMOUS GROUP OF *LAOCOÖN AND HIS SONS* WAS THE WORK OF THE RHODIAN SCULPTORS AGESANDER, ATHENODORUS AND POLYDORUS, WITH MANNERIST FORMS INSPIRED BY THE ART OF PERGAMUM IN THE 1ST CENTURY BC. SCHOLARS ARE STILL DEBATING IF THE WORK IS AN ORIGINAL OR A COPY (VATICAN MUSEUMS, VATICAN CITY).

195 - SOME OF THE MOST IMPORTANT HELLENISTIC SCULPTURAL WORKS COME FROM THE IMPERIAL VILLA AT SPERLONGA. IN PARTICULAR, THE GROTTO-NYMPHAEUM ON THE SEA, WHICH WAS IMAGINED TO BE THE CAVE OF POLYPHEMUS, YIELDED THE FAMOUS GROUP DEPICTING ODYSSEUS BLINDING POLYPHEMUS (THE HEAD IS SHOWN HERE). SCHOLARS HAVE YET TO ESTABLISH IF THE SCULPTURES, ATTRIBUTABLE TO THE RHODIAN SCHOOL, ARE ORIGINALS OR COPIES; DATING RANGES FROM THE 1ST HALF OF THE 1ST CENTURY BC TO THE EARLY 1ST CENTURY AD (ANTIQUARIUM, SPERLONGA).

URBAN PLANNING AND ARCHITECTURE

According to H. Lauter, one of the leading experts on Hellenistic architecture and urban planning, quite often the urban planning of this period was no more than the large-scale implementation – even for smaller towns – of previously tested ideas. Everything revolved around the internal division of the layout according to a road system with ninety-degree intersections, like those of Hippodamus. The new concept of the "metropolis" did not touch Greece, where – in the case of Athens, in any case – work involved integrating and restructuring, generally by enhancing the monumental nature of works. One example is the agora, with its "closed" peristyle effect.

The concept of urban beauty seems to have predominated over criteria of practicality and function. (Architects and urban planners often did not consider topographical difficulties and laid out straight roads that had to cross steep gradients!) Opening up inside the regular city was the square (or several squares) with an impressive architectural system, in which the portico served as the element that regulated and organized built space. The same principles applied to the city's main roads. Unity with the natural landscape was accented. Whenever the lay of the land permitted, a "dramatic" type of urban planning was used, with different terraces that were accessed in stages via grand staircases, and monuments such as theaters whose curved cavea formed a dynamic focal point for the various levels. Pergamum is one of the most impressive examples of this.

During the Archaic and Classical periods large temples dominated the urban landscape, rising over other public buildings and dwellings because of their height or elevated position, with a marked "distance effect." Instead, during Hellenism nearly all public buildings were given a more monumental appearance: administrative and legislative buildings (*bouleuteria, ekklesiasteria*) as well as entertainment structures (theaters), general cultural facilities (gymnasia) and utilitarian ones (such as arsenals and warehouses). Naturally, this also applied to royal palaces, though very little is known about their actual appearance.

The peristyle became an important part of domestic architecture as well. Alongside the construction of classical-style courtyard houses, a type of high-class residence was also developed, featuring a large peristyle courtyard with the various rooms of the house overlooking it. In some cases there were two open spaces, suggesting – based on authoritative sources such as Vitruvius – separate quarters for men and women, or the more likely hypothesis of a family area (*gynaikonitis*) and a representative area (*andronitis*).

The departure from the Classical ideal led to "baroque" concepts in architecture as well, in which – as we have already noted – dramatic, pictorial, animated and intricate effects prevailed over the rational, unitary and static. Above all, the introduction of movement in the layout of the different parts of a building represented the true innovation and a break with the past. The linear arrangement of a façade, for example, was not eliminated but lightened through the interplay of overhangs and recesses, openings and interrup-

tions. In all this, great emphasis was given to what is known as "applied order." In other words, the Classical orders were used to create "faux" architecture that was purely decorative. The use of ephemeral architecture also represented a common trend. These works, which were not designed to endure, were generally erected for important occasions, festivals, processions or celebrations, and were thus made of perishable materials (chiefly wood). Instead, their furnishings were extraordinarily lavish.

196-197 - PERGAMUM IS A FINE EXAMPLE OF HELLENISTIC-ERA URBAN PLANNING. ITS BUILDINGS WERE CONSTRUCTED ON A SERIES OF ARTIFICIAL TERRACES. ACCORDING TO THE GEOGRAPHER STRABO, THE MONUMENTAL LAYOUT OF PERGAMUM WAS COMMISSIONED BY EUMENES II DURING THE 1ST HALF OF THE 2ND CENTURY BC.

197 - DIFFERENT ALTITUDES OF THE TERRAIN WERE EXPLOITED TO HOUSE THE CAVEA OF THE THEATER. THE TERRACES OF THE ACROPOLIS WERE USED FOR ROYAL PALACES, ARSENALS, THE AGORA, THE TEMPLE OF ZEUS AND ATHENA WITH THE GREAT ALTAR, THE TEMPLE OF ATHENA POLIAS, AND OTHER PUBLIC INSTALLATIONS.

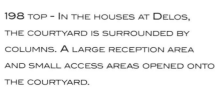

198 TOP - IN THE HOUSES AT DELOS, THE COURTYARD IS SURROUNDED BY COLUMNS. A LARGE RECEPTION AREA AND SMALL ACCESS AREAS OPENED ONTO THE COURTYARD.

198 BOTTOM - THIS MOSAIC, MADE OF STONES, AMPHORA SHARDS AND MARBLE TILES, IS FROM CLEOPATRA'S HOUSE; 130-90 BC.

198-199 - The center of Delos, one of the most important ports of the Hellenistic period, was not constructed based on a single planning concept but expanded through the addition of new quarters.

199 top - The wealthiest houses of Delos were built on the slopes of Mt. Kynthos and around the Sacred Lake. Buildings of several stories were common: the northern part of the dwellings was often elevated to provide better lighting.

199 bottom - The marble lions on the terrace overlooking the Sacred Lake are among the most impressive sculptural works at Delos; late 7th century BC.

APPROACHING THE END

The Third Macedonian War was waged between 171 and 168, between Rome and Perseus, the son of Philip V. At Pydna the consul Lucius Aemilius Paulus defeated the king and took him to Rome as his prisoner, along with an immense amount of booty. (Those deported included the great historian Polybius, who entered the Scipios' sphere of influence and wrote his landmark work, *The Histories* or *The Rise of the Roman Empire*, in Greek.)

The Achaean League stubbornly attempted to resist Roman power, but in 146 Lucius Mummius was routed it at Corinth. He was sacked and destroyed the city, and Greece was merged with Macedon to become a Roman province.

In the Roman culture, admiration for Greek art – fueled by the extraordinary influx of original artwork – sparked the famous ethical-political debate among traditionalists, who leveled the accusation of *luxuria* against those who exploited artwork as private rather than public property, and innovators, who showed openness toward the values that Greek art and civilization contributed to the model of Roman life (*magnificentia*).

In this depleted, devastated and despoiled country, there were violent social disorders, such as the two slave rebellions in Attica in 134 and 100 BC. A series of conflicts swept across the Greek peninsula as well as Asia Minor (the Mithridatic Wars), followed by civil wars: Julius Caesar against Pompey, and Octavian and Mark Antony against Caesar's murderers, followed by the decisive battle between the two victors. Hellenism as a political factor had finally been silenced, and Greek history was merely that of a Roman province.

The decline of republican institutions in Rome and the advent of the new form of imperial power sought by Augustus were accompanied in the provinces by an intense program of glorification and propaganda intended to consolidate dynastic power. The effects of all this were naturally felt in Athens, *domicilium studiorum*. The initial moment of the Athenian program came with Augustus' encounter with King Phraates IV of Parthia in 20 BC. Along with the return of the Roman insignias lost by Crassus, this encounter temporarily brought wars to an end in this part of the world. This event evoked the Greek success over the Persians (which imperial propaganda presented as the ancestors of the Parthians) four centuries before. At the same time, it was also a veiled allusion to Alexander the Great, the figure whom Augustus had always aspired to imitate.

On the Acropolis, directly across from the east façade of the Parthenon, a small round temple was built by the *demos*, the people, and dedicated to the cult of Rome and Augustus, who was indicated as the "savior" (*soter*). This small building was thus highly significant: in a key area of the religious landscape of Athens and, indeed, all of Greece, it sealed a power that transcended the human level. Two equally significant monuments were also built in the middle of the clearing of the agora, the city's political hub and the symbol of Hellenism: the Odeon of Agrippa, a tribute to Athens' cultural supremacy, but also the deliberate occupation of the central area of the city's political and economic life with a monument dedicated to spectacle; the Temple of Ares / Mars, a 5th-century building that was dismantled from a site in the Attic countryside, transported and reassembled here in 2 BC. Dedicated to Gaius Caesar, Augustus' designated successor (who met his untimely death in AD 4), its purpose was magnificent dynastic celebration. The construction of a temple dedicated to Hermes Agoraios on the west side of the square completed the program. In addition to the creation – or completion – of the Roman agora, other works, chiefly restorations, accompanied several dedications by Athens' ruling class, as a sign of loyalty toward the new power.

As a man of culture, Augustus (like most Roman intellectuals) viewed Athens as his standard, and classicism fully suited a model of propaganda that strived to create the appearance of a "golden age." An emblematic image of the emperor can be seen in the statue *Augustus Prima Porta*, which portrays the *princeps* in a cuirass as he addresses his army. This work is clearly modeled after Polyclitus' *Doryphorus*, one of the highest expressions of the Classical period!

201

201 - THIS SECTION OF THE SARCOPHAGUS MADE OF LUNI MARBLE PORTRAYS A BATTLE BETWEEN THE GREEKS AND THE ASIANS; 2ND CENTURY AD (ARCHAEOLOGICAL MUSEUM, BRESCIA).

THE LEGACY OF GREECE

The term "classical" has two souls: Greek and Roman. The history of the Roman world seems to aspire to the condition of universal history, and yet the strongest claims to the universality and perpetual validity of the "classical" world actually come from tiny Greece. Despite its immense power, Rome comes across as a mere mediator of Greek culture. As a result, during the modern age countries that during the "classical" period had little or nothing to do with the Greeks and knew very little about them – Germany and England, for example – wanted to link their roots to those of the Greeks.

During the Roman era, classicism played the pivotal role of merging the past, creating a global yet eclectic image of Greek art: a fully "cultured" art, as opposed to what was happening in Rome and the Italian peninsula, the West and various parts of the Middle East, such as Egypt, where a "popular" or "plebeian" level – in short, "uncultured" art – flourished.

With the fall of the Roman Empire, almost all knowledge was lost, not only of art but above all of Greek culture, starting with its most important medium: language. Greek continued to be spoken only in the Byzantine area. Nevertheless, there is no doubt about the fact that the legacy of ancient Greece was handed down to many fields of science. It is documented not only by written and illustrated texts, but also by the existence of scientific instruments such as astrolabes, goniometers (direction finders), sundials, scales, surgical instruments and mucha more.

The revival of Greek culture did not occur in the Western world until the advent of Humanism and the Renaissance. In the meantime, however, the Greek legacy made enormous contributions to the Arab culture. The spread of scientific and philosophical knowledge had far-reaching effects, and it came about in a number of ways, including the translation of texts. Notably, the new Islamic culture spread to much of the area that, during the Hellenistic period, had been home to populations whose cultural, social, economic and institutional traditions – and thus also their scientific legacy – were Greek. The Arabic translations of Euclid's *Elements* and *Optics*, Archimedes' *On the Measurement of the Circle*, Ptolemy's *Optics*, Apollonius' *Conics*, and Anthemius' *Mechanical Paradoxes*

are famous. The seminal thirteen-book *Arithmetica* by Diophantus of Alexandria (2nd century BC) was the basis of Al-KhwÇrizmi's *Algebra*. Ptolemy, who wrote the most complete treatise on astronomy, gave the Arab culture the *Almagest*, or *The Great Treatise* (*Megale Syntaxis*). In the field of biology, the works of Galen (medicine) and Aristotle (natural philosophy) had enormous influence on the works of Avicenna.

In the field of art, this encounter with the Greek world was inevitable and took on different forms at different times. It ranged from the use of spolia ("spoils": e.g., columns and capitals from Greek temple were incorporated into mosques) to crafts (glassmaking), decoration techniques (mosaics), and the illustration of books. In the West, between the late 15th and the early 16th centuries traces of the perception of Greek art as an objective reality and not a literary "phantom" appeared in several collections – mainly in the Veneto area of Italy – with a handful of items mainly from Rhodes, Cyprus and Crete. In 1506, the discovery in Rome of the statue of *Laocoön and His Sons*, by the Rhodian sculptors Agesander, Polydorus and Athenodorus, was an epochal event. For a long time, however, Greek art was manifested mainly in the form of Roman reproductions, most of which were not even acknowledged as such. The main criterion used for identifying and evaluating the artwork of the past was quality: anything exceedingly beautiful and precious could only be Greek. It was not until the mid-18th century that the great German scholar J. J. Winckelmann effectively "discovered" Greek art. This "discovery" was made within the limitations of Roman documentation, but a new door had been opened. The style was analyzed, the works were organized according to periods and chronological phases, and history of ancient art was established. The ambiguity of originals/copies would later be overcome through what we can refer to as archeological philology, recovering and reconstructing original documents and images.

Nevertheless, a certain bias remains, and the idea that the entire Greek civilization is represented by 5th-century Athens still influences scholarship and, above all, our common mindset. This is one of the reasons for this book.

203 - RAPHAEL'S *THE SCHOOL OF ATHENS* (1509) – A RENAISSANCE MASTERPIECE – PORTRAYS THE MOST IMPORTANT PHILOSOPHERS OF ANCIENT GREECE AS THEY DEBATE INSIDE A CLASSICAL BUILDING. PLATO AND ARISTOTLE ARE DEPICTED IN THE MIDDLE OF THE FRESCO, WHICH DECORATES THE STANZA DELLE SEGNATURE AT THE VATICAN MUSEUMS.

BIBLIOGRAPHY

General references:
M.I.FINLEY, Uso e abuso della storia. Il significato, lo studio e la comprensione del passato, Turin
S.SETTIS (a cura di), I Greci. Storia Cultura Arte Società, I - ..., Turin 1996 - ...
S.SETTIS, Futuro del classico, Turin 2004.
History:
M.I.FINLEY, La democrazia degli antichi e dei moderni, Rome-Bari 1973
N.G.L.HAMMOND, A History of Greece, Oxford 1973.
D.MUSTI, Storia greca, Bari 1999.
Art History:
Enciclopedia dell'Arte Antica Classica e Orientale, I - ..., Rome 1958 - ...
M.ROBERTSON, A History of Greek Art, I-II, Cambridge 1975.
A.GIULIANO, Storia dell'arte greca, Rome 1989.
Lexicon Iconographicum Mythologiae Classicae, I - ..., Zurich-Munich, 1981 - ...

208 - THE ATHENA OF PIRAEUS IS A BRONZE STATUE FROM THE MID-4TH CENTURY BC AND IT PORTRAYS THE GODDESS WITH A PLUMED HELMET (ARCHAEOLOGICAL MUSEUM OF PIRAEUS, ATHENS).

Q 938 Mag
Maggi, Stefano.
Greece